UNLOCK

12 keys to

THE POWER OF

health, happiness and success

YOU

TERRY WILDEMANN

and other experts

AVIVA
PUBLISHING
NEW YORK

Unlock the Power of YOU: 12 Keys to Health, Happiness & Success

Published by:
Aviva Publishing
2301 Saranac Avenue
Lake Placid, NY 12946
518-523-1320
www.avivapubs.com

Disclaimer: This book is a compilation of ideas from numerous experts who have each contributed a chapter. As such, the views expressed in each chapter are those of each author and not necessarily of Aviva Publishing or the other experts in the book.

Compiled by Susan A. Friedmann of Aviva Publishing,
www.avivapubs.com

Project management and editing by Doug Wagner and Toni Robino of Windword Literary Services, www.WindwordLiteraryServices.com

Cover Design by Yael Halpern of Halpern Designs,
www.halperndesigns.com

Page Design & Layout by Fusion Creative Works, www.fusioncw.com

ISBN 978-1-938686-20-7

Printed in the United States of America

Additional copies of

Unlock the Power of YOU: 12 Keys to Health, Happiness & Success can be obtained from any of the authors by contacting them directly.

Quantity discounts are available through the publisher.

Contents

Foreword   5

    by Michael J. Losier, author of *Law of Attraction*
    and *Law of Connection*

Introduction   7

    by Susan A. Friedmann, author of
    Riches in Niches

Chapter One   9

    Breaking Free From the Prison of Your Mind
    by Susan A. Friedmann

Chapter Two   27

    The Power of Clarity and Focus
    by Carol Stringham

Chapter Three   43

    Laying Your Soul Foundation
    by Laura Murphy

Chapter Four   59

    Optimal Health: It's not what you think or do;
    it's who you become
    by Dr. Bruce Hoffman

Chapter Five   **75**

    Happiness Attracts Success

    by Conrad Toner

Chapter Six   **91**

    Finding Happiness When Life Is a Mess

    by Judy Palmer

Chapter Seven   **109**

    Go For the Goal!

    by Peter Scott Stringham

Chapter Eight   **125**

    Attracting Your Ideal Weight

    by Zaheen Nanji

Chapter Nine   **141**

    Moving Ahead With Zero-Based Thinking

    by Paul V. Xavier

Chapter Ten   **157**

    Soul Care for Stressed Superwomen

    by Jolina Karen

Chapter Eleven   **173**

    Create Heart Centered Prosperity

    by Terry Wildemann

Chapter Twelve   **191**

    Unlocking Your Power of Perception

    by Jeffrey Ferrazzo

Foreword

by Michael J. Losier

Have you ever noticed that some people seem to be living under a dark cloud while for others the sun is always shining? Have you wondered why people who are grateful and joyful tend to be healthier and more successful than people who complain all the time? Contrary to popular belief, it's not luck. It's energy. We don't get what we think we deserve. We get what our energy field attracts. According to the Law of Attraction, when it comes to our energy and vibration, like attracts like.

While this concept may be new to you and is sometimes dismissed as "New Age," it's been covered in books for at least a century. *Thought Vibration or the Law of Attraction in the Thought World,* by William Walter Atkinson, was published in 1906. My own interest in the Law of Attraction was sparked when I studied neuro-linguistic programming in 1995. NLP looks at how our thoughts and words affect our behavior. The idea that my thinking created a vibrational field (commonly called our "vibe") was a big wake-up call for me, and I hope it is for you, too.

What this means is that by changing your thoughts and behavioral patterns, you can change your reality. No matter what's happening in your life or how daunting your challenges may be, you have the power to attract more of what you want and less of what you don't want. As humans, we tend to think this is too easy or sounds too good to be true. I know I had those doubts at first. But when I put it to the test in my own life, magic started to happen. What I had previously written off as pipe dreams were suddenly within reach, and before I knew it, one by one, these cherished dreams began coming true.

But you don't need to take my word for it. You can prove it yourself. This book will give you the keys to unlock the power you already possess to be healthier, happier and more successful. Written by some of North America's leading authorities, *Unlock the Power of YOU* offers principles, strategies and exercises all designed to open the door to your wildest dreams.

– Michael J. Losier
Author of *Law of Attraction*
and *Law of Connection*

Introduction

by Susan A. Friedmann

You already have the innate ability to unlock the power of *you*. All you need are the keys. And this book hands them to you. It's packed full of inspirational and practical advice to challenge old beliefs, robotic behaviors, habits and patterns that no longer serve you. The authors offer you powerful techniques, guidance and golden nuggets for tapping into the highest possible level of life balance, health, happiness, inner peace and success.

Unlock the Power of YOU shows you how to maximize personal potential by harnessing sustainable long-term change and taking advantage of the powerful source of infinite energy that exists within each of us.

If you're willing to learn a few simple techniques and let go of some old ways of thinking, you can unlock your power to make profound changes in your life—no matter what your circumstances and no matter how impossible it may seem to you right now.

Once you have the keys, you can immediately start driving your life in the direction that's most inspiring and joyful to you. You can attract the opportunities and experiences you desire, follow your innermost dreams and enjoy the miracle of life.

> – Susan A. Friedmann
> The NichePreneur Coach
> Lake Placid, N.Y.

CHAPTER ONE

Breaking Free From the Prison of Your Mind

by Susan A. Friedmann

From earliest memory, my small world was a prison. The first seven years of my life, I awoke to the sight of metal bars across my bedroom window. They weren't there to hold me captive; they were there to prevent me from falling from the eighth floor of our apartment building in London. But I found them confining nonetheless.

Freedom came, in part, when my family moved to a four-bedroom house in the suburbs with a sizable garden backing onto a beautiful tree-lined park. My large bedroom window treated me to miles of rolling emerald-green hills, beckoning me to come out and play.

But because of my poor grades in essay writing, every weekend my father assigned me a writing project. Sometimes this took a few hours and other times it took the entire weekend. Once again my bedroom was my prison. The freedom I yearned for was put on hold until the assignment was deemed satisfactory.

Although my imprisonment was distressing, at least it was temporary. Damon, on the other hand, has been behind bars for 20 years, incarcerated for gun and drug possession. With his release date ten years away, his freedom is very much on hold. At 40 years old, with a third-grade reading ability, he recognizes the bad choices he's made and vows that, on his release, he will make a brand-new crime-free life for himself.

For six years, as a literacy volunteer, I helped Damon with his reading and writing. It was this weekly encounter that motivated me to think of my life in a different way. My awareness and perception changed every time I found myself inside his walled city. It forced me to think about the choices I've made in life, the many times I've held myself hostage with obsessive or paralyzing thoughts. Thoughts that came—and still come—in the form of a critical and judgmental voice inside my mind, trying to stop me from stepping into my own power and greatness. Unlike the steel bars that hold Damon back, my barriers are constructed of my own thoughts. Fortunately, I have the opportunity to choose how I approach my world.

How about you? Do you live in similar captivity? How often do you put a wall around yourself to keep others out? How often do you stop yourself from doing something you'd love to do?

Recently, I realized that the chatter in my mind has no power without my consent. It's just a collection of ideas, beliefs, comments, explanations, judgments, worries, fears, fantasies and dreams. They are based completely on my experience of the world and the people who have influenced me the most.

I know that this critical voice sometimes guides me into savvy decision-making, but more often it presents nasty irrational beliefs that ridicule me about the choices I've made. This voice spews out humiliation, criticisms and reminders that I'm not good enough. I'm a failure. It judges and disapproves of the way I live my life. It convicts me and sentences me to prison.

How about you? How often do you confine yourself and allow thoughts to imprison you? What choices are you making that amplify the inner-critic voice or make it more persistent?

For many people, struggle, restlessness and unhappiness go hand in hand with living. They're rarely happy, because they're constantly wanting something they don't have.

Yvonne, someone I've known for years, never seems happy. When I see her, she complains about her family and friends or something she's bought that isn't quite right. She constantly craves more stuff, and as she satisfies one want, a new one quickly takes its place. She has short-lived moments of happiness with each new purchase, but then the vicious circle of unhappiness begins again. Her conditioned thinking is that something or someone in the future will liberate her and present her with long-lasting freedom and bliss.

YOUR PRISON VOICE

I call the negative internal voice "the prison voice." Part-warden and part-trickster, this powerful beast lives and thrives by toying with our subconscious while at the same time professing to be our protector and friend.

The Warden:

As a warden, your inner critic protects and makes certain you come to as little harm as possible. It judges what's good, bad, acceptable, unacceptable, believable or ridiculous. It helps you avoid taking risks, sounds danger signals, holds you back and steers you clear of rejection, embarrassment, and emotional and physical pain. However, this prison voice also stands in the way of your fully experiencing love, joy and success, limiting rather than empowering you. In essence, it forbids your true self from enjoying life to the fullest.

The Trickster:

As a trickster, your inner critic is extremely skillful and forceful at pretending it's the voice of knowledge, reason and wisdom. It works hard to provide you with a sense of security, keeping you safe, comfortable and closeted within the walls of the status quo. It convinces you that this is for your own good, and tricks you into believing that worry, anxiety and guilt have true value. You put trust in myths such as "You're better off only enjoying yourself for brief periods," "Asking for what you want is selfish," "Not expressing feelings will make them go away" or "You're fat, stupid, a failure, or undeserving of love."

The trickster also likes to give you an anxiety attack every now and then. It feeds your subconscious fears so covertly that you don't even know why you're afraid or paralyzed to move forward in your life even though you have a strong conscious desire to do so. It discourages you from exploring new ideas with its "should nots," "must nots" and "cannots." It manipulates you into feeling worthless, afraid, not good enough and incapable of reaching specific goals.

Together, the warden and the trickster play havoc, keeping you imprisoned and planting negative beliefs that blossom into self-doubt and fears, particularly when you're most vulnerable.

Whether we like it or not, we all have this prison voice lurking in our subconscious. It's the combined voices of parents, colleagues, friends, enemies and strangers we've met along life's journey. Though the prison voice can protect us from embarrassment and failure, listening to it can also stop us from reaching our maximum potential. While the voice certainly serves us in many ways, the key to moving forward in our lives is to learn to manage it instead of letting it manage us.

IDENTIFY AND RECORD YOUR PRISON VOICE

Take a moment to write down three times in your life when you allowed your prison voice (warden or trickster) to stand in the way of doing what you really wanted to do, because it was safer, you felt undeserving or helpless, or it was just the easiest way out.

BREAKING FREE

So how can you knock down your prison walls and set yourself free from your obsessive thoughts and irrational beliefs? How can you avoid fears of failure, success, risk or not being perfect that stand between you and your freedom, power and greatness? How can you use memories and thoughts intelligently without allowing them to trap you and fence you in?

To unlock the doors of your mind and break free to new ways of thinking and behaving, you need a master key. Imagine a powerful, dynamic and vital tool that opens up a world of infinite possibilities. How would you feel being in charge, taking control and complete responsibility for the choices you make, good or bad, wise or foolish? This key to freedom shapes your fate or fortune and enhances your ability to move forward in the direction of your choice.

Plain and simple, you are the master of your destiny. This simple key is often hard to use because taking on the tremendous responsibility of your life can be as scary as it is exhilarating. Each day of your life is open to countless possibilities and opportunities, but it's tough to continually avoid the trap of blaming others and feeling helpless and stuck. If you're like most people, there are probably days when it's a cinch to unlock your door to freedom and others when your key just doesn't fit the lock. When this happens, you need three tools to help you ace your escape.

CRACK THE CODE TO ACE YOUR ESCAPE

Let me introduce you to the three tools that will help you control the prison voice and turn your walls of permanent concrete into easy-to-tear paper you can walk through at will. I'm talking about Awareness, Choice and Experience.

AWARENESS

Awareness is your key to recognizing, understanding, working, shaping and transforming the old you into the new you. Before you can gain control of your prison voice, you need to master and harness the power of now.

Worrying obsessively about future unknowns and feeling guilty or resentful about the past only distracts you from being present in the now. According to transformation guru Eckhart Tolle, author of *The Power of Now: A Guide to Spiritual Enlightenment*, "To make the journey into The Power of Now, we need to leave our analytical mind and its false created self, the ego, behind. Virtually everyone hears a voice, or several voices, continuous monologues and dialogues."

Being in the now is all about total awareness of your surroundings and yourself in that environment. Stop right now and listen to the voice in your head. Pay special attention to the phrases or sentences that frequently repeat themselves.

When we listen to that voice, our goal is to detach from any emotional reaction. Rather than getting angry or sad when you notice it, simply learn to hear it as you would if the voice were on television talking to someone other than you. With practice, you will be able to separate yourself and your true voice from the prison voice. "When you listen to a thought, you are aware not only of the thought but also of yourself as the witness of the thought," Tolle says. "A new dimension of consciousness has come. As you listen to the thought, you feel a conscious presence—your deeper self—behind or underneath the thought. The thought then loses its power over you and quickly subsides, because you are no longer energizing the mind through identification with it. This is the beginning of the end of involuntary and compulsive thinking."

Documenting Your Prison Voice

Find a nice quiet spot away from distractions. Close your eyes and listen to the noise and chatter in your mind. What are you hearing and feeling? What irrational thoughts and beliefs are vying for your attention? Once you've identified them, tune in to how they make you feel. Then do a brain dump and write down whatever comes into your mind, sensible or irrational. This is for your eyes only!

Noticing and Recording Your Feelings

For the next seven days, take five to 10 minutes each day to write down how you feel when you're …

Day 1: By yourself

Day 2: With a friend

Day 3: With a stranger

Day 4: With your boss

Day 5: With your parents

Day 6: With your partner

Day 7: With each of your children, grandchildren, nephews or nieces

The more aware you are about the feelings that well up inside you when you're with various people in your life, the better able you are to take control of your prison thoughts as they happen.

CHOICE

Once you've gained the awareness and are more mindful of your thoughts, you're ready for your next tool: Choice.

As adults, we make choices all day long about how we act and how we feel. Some action choices are easy, routine and mindless, such as getting up, showering and brushing our teeth. Other choices are more difficult and require more thought, such as the amount of freedom we give to our children, whom we vote for in an election and which battles are worth fighting. We love it when we hear accolades for the good choices, but how many times do we shun taking responsibility for bad choices, preferring to blame others for any negative outcomes.

Even more challenging are our feeling choices and taking responsibility for the myriad emotions or moods that occur daily. For example, we can choose to be sad, depressed or frustrated, angry, aggravated or cranky, happy, motivated or inspired—the choice is totally ours.

I'll let you in on a little secret: When I have an important event to attend, it often takes several clothing changes and lots of parading in front of the mirror before I can make a final decision. I frequently think I don't have the right thing to wear, despite having a well-stocked wardrobe. Inevitably, once I've made up my mind and I'm on my way to the event, my prison voice informs me, "You should have worn something else." Immediately, I feel overdressed or underdressed for the occasion. The prison voice sees an opening and taunts me, "Everyone will be wearing the right thing except you." How ridiculous is that?! This is when I get the opportunity to tell the prison voice to take a hike.

On the road of choices, you'll frequently come to a crossroads with one signpost pointing to the path of thoughtlessness and the other to the path of thoughtfulness. Like it or not, you're totally in charge of the direction you choose.

Choose the thoughtlessness path and you've just opted to hand your control over to your prison voice. This is when you hear messages like "I knew it wouldn't work, "I can't do anything about it," "I'd better not rock the boat," "I need help," "I'll never forgive that person" and "I'm upset, so it's okay to have some chocolate." Which of these sound familiar?

Alternatively, choose the thoughtfulness path and you're the master of your destiny, in charge of how you think, feel and act. Pure and simple, good thoughts make you feel good and bad thoughts make you feel lousy.

Choice gives you the chance to have control over your life. The more aware of the choices you make, the more control you have over the outcomes. As television celebrity Oprah Winfrey says, "Understand that the right to choose your own path is a sacred privilege. Use it. Dwell in possibility."

COLLECTING THE EVIDENCE

List three choices you made in the last few weeks where you followed the thoughtfulness path and ended up being proud of your accomplishments.

Next, list three choices you made where you regret following the thoughtlessness path.

EXPERIENCE

Now that you're familiar with awareness and choice, it's time to receive the third and final tool to ace your escape: Experience.

Your life is filled to the brim with experiences from birth to the grave. The choices you make inevitably lead to outcomes, some positive and some negative. It's your life experiences that build the self-confidence, self-esteem and overall strength and perseverance that allow you to enjoy the journey.

"If you collect a lifetime of negative beliefs about your own abilities, you'll tend to have low self-confidence, unless you do something about it," says transformational psychologist Dr. Jill Ammon-Wexler. "Doing something about it starts with the recognition that *you* are in charge. Self-confidence is a vital ingredient of happiness. Without it you often won't even try to do or be what you are really capable of."

Navigating your life's journey means vigilantly watching for signs that your prison voice is stealing your enjoyment of an experience. Signs such as fear, hopelessness, depression, guilt, anger, blame, frustration, impatience and jealousy can mean you're being held in a prison cell.

Instead, become familiar with your inner wisdom, a voice that helps you trust yourself to know when something is right or wrong. Often known as intuition or a "gut feeling" about something, this instinct or sixth sense helps guide you through life's experience maze.

I remember accompanying my husband, Alec, for a job interview in Corpus Christi, Texas, several years ago. We were wined, dined and made to feel as if the job was his for the taking. However, when our host dropped us off at the airport, the way she said, "Take care," hit me in the gut. I can still remember the feeling. I instinctively knew she was really saying goodbye and we were not moving to Texas. I was right. Several days later, Alec learned that the committee had chosen another candidate for the job.

EMBRACING YOUR POWER

Write down three experiences that made you feel powerful and three times you had a "gut feeling" about something, whether you acted on it or not.

TAKING RESPONSIBILITY

Now that you have the tools, you have the opportunity to choose your experience. These extraordinarily powerful tools are yours to use to subdue the prison voice and free your mind. It's unlikely that you'll get rid of the prison voice forever, but these tools will give you the power to diminish their strength and loosen the stranglehold on you. You have the authority and responsibility to break free and step into your power to accept your own greatness.

"Choosing to live in the absolute perfection of who you truly are, leads you to the Master Key that opens any door," says Debra Oakland, author of *Living in Courage*. "The potential hidden within each of us is staggering. Shed the old layers. Devote yourself to something of value that sings to the passion in your soul. Now you become the master of your destiny."

Wishing you much strength and courage
to be all that you can be!

About the Author

Susan A. Friedmann

Susan Friedmann, CSP (certified speaking professional), The NichePreneur™ Coach, is an internationally recognized niche-marketing expert and "how to" coach who helps entrepreneurs, small-business owners and service professionals maximize opportunities to improve results and focus on building better relationships with customers, prospects and advocates in the marketplace.

A prolific author, Susan has written twelve books, including *Riches in Niches: How to Make It BIG in a Small Market* (made

No. 1 in hot business books on Amazon.com), *Meeting and Event Planning for Dummies* and *The Complete Idiot's Guide to Target Marketing.* Many of Susan's books have been translated into several languages, and her training materials are used worldwide. She has appeared on a variety of radio talk shows and as a guest expert on CNN's Financial Network and *Bloomberg's Small Business.*

One of only 200 women to hold the National Speakers Association's highest earned designation of certified speaking professional, she has proven platform experience and knows how to deliver top-notch presentations designed to inform, excite and motivate groups of every size.

www.richesinniches.com

THE
NiCHEPRENEUR
COACH

Stand Out in a Crowded Marketplace

If you're like most people in business, chances are good that you face some challenges. Given the pace of today's world and the unbelievable mass of information and misinformation available, it's never been easier to "get lost down a rabbit hole" only to come back out feeling confused and overwhelmed. As you struggle for more sales, you don't have enough time to really enjoy your life.

And it's certainly not your fault if you feel this way. There are more than thousands of others around the globe who experience the same kinds of challenges and are desperate for all the help they can get.

Take a long, deep breath because we're going to take aim at these challenges.

"Discover the Secrets to Building a Business That Attracts Customers Who *REALLY* Want to Buy What You Sell" is a *free* 45-minute no-nonsense webinar packed with simple, practical and immediately useful, tips, tricks and tools that can be almost shockingly powerful. It's all aimed at helping you overcome the challenges that are holding you back from achieving the success you strive for in your business and your life.

To sign up for this must-attend webinar: just go to http://richesinniches.com/webinar and choose the date and time that work best for you.

THE NICHEPRENEUR COACH

Helping you find the right niche market
for your business success

http://richesinniches.com

susan@richesinniches.com

CHAPTER TWO

The Power of Clarity and Focus

by Carol Stringham

While I was on a hike in the White Mountains of New Hampshire, the sun was high in the sky and I marveled at the beauty that encompassed me. As I hiked along the Mount Tecumseh trail, evergreens and the scent of pine surrounded me, and when I rounded a bend, I saw a hawk soaring in big slow circles. It was hot, but the air was fresh and I was loving every minute. I felt calm, centered and happy. When I reached the halfway point on the descent, I stopped to have a snack and discovered that I had only a few sips of water left in my water bottle. Much to my chagrin, my energetic teenage sons, whom I had suggested go ahead, had the reserve supply. I was suddenly very thirsty. I knew that if I ran out of water, I'd make it the remaining mile back to the car and be fine, but being hyper-aware of my thirst became an annoying distraction. I saw a bush bursting with small delicate blueberries on the trail, but I didn't appreciate it. I heard the white-throated sparrow's melodious whistle pierce the air, but I didn't stop to enjoy it. I was focusing on what I didn't have and I felt drained, tired and cranky.

Our energy supply for life is a lot like the water supply on my hike, but on a much larger scale. When our life-energy reservoir is full of fine water, we have all the energy we need and we enjoy the inner peace and freedom that it brings. When the reservoir is running dry, we feel depleted and fear that we won't have what we need to survive. Many people don't give much thought to this energy reservoir even though we all draw from it every day. How full the reservoir is and how often it's replenished depend on how well we express and honor ourselves. Over time, even little leaks in our reservoir will deplete the supply, giving us less to draw on and curtailing our freedom of choice.

What's incredible is that once we know how to keep the reservoir full and the energy flowing, we can do just about anything. But first, we have to be clear about what we want.

SNAPSHOT LIFE ASSESSMENT

Right now, take an assessment of your life by writing your answers to the following questions. Our thoughts are fast and fleeting, and writing them down captures more specific information. Writing your answers can also lead you to fresh perspectives and increase your accountability to yourself.

1. Am I getting what I want in life?

2. What am I most dissatisfied about? What do I keep complaining about?

3. What negative stories do I keep repeating to my friends and family?

4. Do I expose vulnerable parts of myself in order to make more of myself known?

5. Do I let people know what I really want, or do I keep it to myself?

6. Am I directly asking for what I want or am I covert about it?

7. Do I clearly state my boundaries with a clear "yes" and "no"?

THE ART OF ASKING DIRECTLY

Do you hint at what you want or hope that others can read your mind? If so, you probably already know that it doesn't work so well. I'm inviting you to start being more precise. "*Will* you bring me a glass of water?" is a different question from "*Can* you bring me a glass of water?" And it's a world away from simply saying, "I'm thirsty," and hoping someone will bring you a glass of water.

The words *can* and *could* refer to ability, so most people can say "yes" to a question that begins with *can* or *could*. The person you're asking doesn't have to do anything beyond answering the question, because you haven't made a specific request or gotten his or her agreement. It's like casting a line to catch a fish without using bait or a hook. Good luck catching that fish! On the other hand, when you ask "*will* you?" or "*would* you?"

you're asking whether someone wants to form an agreement with you. If he or she says "yes," the agreement is formed.

In an effort to be polite, people sometimes say "*will* you?" when they're giving a command, rather than actually giving you a choice. When the boss says, "Will you set up a meeting for me with the director?" she is really saying, "Set up the meeting." I learned an important lesson about when to ask and when to tell from a kindergartner. I approached Tommy in class as he was assembling a wooden building. I gave him a choice when I asked, "Will you come with me for testing?" He continued playing and said "no." I realized my communication mistake and had to honor his response. I waited for him to complete his Empire State Building before commanding, "It's time to come with me now." If I had used this command initially, it would have been much more effective. However, if I had insisted on his following me to the testing after having initially given him a choice, he would have learned not to trust me.

There are many ways to avoid directly asking for what we want. When my client Mary didn't get an engagement ring after hinting and complaining to her fiancé for months, she pleaded her case to his cat while it was curled up in his lap. And when my client Nancy was afraid her husband wouldn't want to go to the newborn-baby class with her, she demanded that he accompany her instead of inviting him. He got angry, dug in his heels and said he had to work late. This was a pattern in their relationship until she realized that she wasn't giving him a chance to willingly say "yes." There are many ways we can get our signals crossed when we're talking with one another.

Using a direct and respectful approach increases our chances of understanding and being understood.

WHAT I WANT BUT HAVEN'T ASKED FOR

Draw two lines down a sheet of paper to make three vertical columns. In the left column, make a list of what you want but haven't asked for. In the middle column, identify the action needed to get what you've listed in the left column. In the right column, write the names of those you will ask for what you want.

Example:

Left column: I want my sons to put their clean clothes away and their dirty clothes in the hamper.

Middle column: Ask for clean clothes to be put away and dirty clothes to be put in the hamper

Right column: My sons

If you complete this exercise and select one or two items to directly ask for each week, within a month you will be amazed by how much energy you have. Your reservoir will fill up quickly when you honor yourself.

My friend Judy, who owns and runs a prosperous graphic design business, used this form when she reached the end of her rope with her husband and kids. She was exhausted because she didn't trust anyone enough to delegate and didn't feel safe enough to ask her husband and kids for help. Instead, she had fallen into the habit of complaining instead of directly asking. She was angry and bitter. She looked as if her energy reservoir had been dry for quite some time. Doing this exercise was a big reality check for her. She realized that she'd stopped asking for help because she didn't think she'd get it and because she thought she should be able to do everything herself. This kind of thinking made her alone and miserable. She used this tool to re-engage with her husband and kids, and she was surprised by how willing they were to do what she asked of them. Needless to say, the entire family benefited from the courageous shift she made.

Be clear and specific about what you want, and practice asking for it directly. If the person you ask agrees to fulfill your request but doesn't do so or doesn't do so in the manner you had envisioned, try to figure out where the communication broke down so you can put the correction in. Think about how you can be more specific or precise the next time you make a request. By being direct and clear, you increase your chances of getting what you want and you conserve the energy in your reservoir.

One sure way to deplete your energy supply is to get trapped in the "why" cage. "Why is this happening to me?" is not a helpful question. It keeps your focus in the past and triggers your mind to fixate on all the reasons you didn't get what you wanted. Instead, turn your attention to getting the results you want by asking questions that begin with *how* and *what*. "How can I achieve this goal?" "What do I need to do next?"

When you ask people directly for what you want and you get it, you start to become more open to possibilities, more permeable. Being open and clear about what you want and asking for it takes courage and a willingness to be vulnerable. But if you want others to support your true desires, you have to be willing to ask and make yourself known. Learning to ask and receive is just as valuable as learning to give and be responsive. This give-and-take in relationships is what makes life work.

Keep in mind that just as you want the freedom to say "yes" or "no," so do other people. Every day, we all say "yes" to some options and "no" to others. When we say "yes," we're enrolling in the opportunity. When we say "no," we're energetically disengaging from one option and creating space for something else. But if we sit the fence, choosing neither "yes" nor "no," we're using up energy that we could be directing to something we know we want. There is power only in "yes" and "no." Anything in between drains our energy and the energy of others. This is true even with small choices, such as whether to attend an event. If a friend invites you to a dinner party, the instant you say "yes" or "no," you both act accordingly. But until you respond, you and your friend use energy to maintain the holding pattern. It's like treading water. Conversely, when you respond with a clear "yes" or "no," it allows you and your friend to move forward, energetically unburdened.

DOUBT AS AN ALLY

Have you ever noticed that when you make a big decision, it's often followed by doubt? We can use this doubt as an ally to confirm that we've made a decision. To decide means to cut off. When we experience doubt about a choice we've made, we can either re-commit to the "yes" or commit to the doubt. When we find ourselves at a crossroads like this, it's important to check in and ask, "Which action will move me closer to what I want?"

When you commit to a goal that feels like a big stretch, you will face challenges and experience some discomfort. But guess what—if you commit to the doubt, you're also going to face challenges and experience discomfort. Stretching leads to growth and improvement. Doubting leads to stagnation and self-recrimination.

Many people break commitments because they are disempowered by their doubt and quit before they have a chance to discover whether they can do what the commitment requires. When we do this, it weakens our life energy and lowers our self-value. But how do we know whether we're getting in over our heads?

My son faced this question when he decided to play high school football. He knew that the schedule would be grueling and that being on the team would be a big commitment on his and his parents' part. Within two days, he started complaining that he didn't like the difficult training schedule. On the second day, he told me that being a football player was not what he wanted after all. I informed him that it was too late because he had already made a choice. I said he could decide if he wanted to be on next year's team after experiencing the full season he'd enrolled in this year. Holding my son to this commitment strengthened his ability to make good choices. If he had not kept his commitment to complete one season on the football team, he wouldn't have found out how he really felt about playing. In the end, he finished the season, rejoined the following year and was asked to be captain.

I'd shared the same suggestion with him as I do with my clients: If an opportunity presents itself and it's not an absolute "yes," your answer should probably be "no." It's not that commitments should never be broken—sometimes that's the best choice—but when we do this, we have to take responsibility for the way our choice will affect the other person or people involved. And to maintain our integrity and the water in our reservoir, we have to reach an agreement about how restitution will be made. Most people are willing to negotiate, especially when you can make it a win for them, too.

For example, when my friend Susan accepted a full-time job even though she didn't want to work more than 20 hours a week, she knew she'd made a mistake. She was a new mom, and her fear of losing the job opportunity had propelled her to agree to the full-time offer. But by the time she got home, she was furious with herself and seeing red. Within a few hours she developed pinkeye, not wanting to see what she had done. She realized she wasn't being true to herself and decided to ask for a part-time position, even if it meant not getting the job at all. After making this decision to meet with her boss about the part-time position, her eyes cleared. She apologized for her initial response and explained that the position had been posted as part time when she applied and part time was what she wanted. She was delighted to learn that the position could be split so that she could work part time.

REFRAME YOUR NEGATIVE THOUGHTS

The universe reflects back to us measure for measure what we put into it. Watch the words you speak. Did you ever notice that whatever you pay attention to, you get more of? Often, people say what they don't want but neglect to say what they do want. They get caught up in their story, focus on their limitations and make excuses for not getting what they want. In the process, they use an enormous amount of energy making themselves miserable. And they can be energy drains on the people around them, too.

Unfortunately, people who do this usually don't realize that they're making their lives more difficult. Focusing on what they don't want and blaming other people or circumstances for their plight has become a way of life for them. This was the case with my client Ernie. We were having a dinner meeting at an upscale Italian restaurant that had just opened. As we were waiting to be seated, Ernie said, "I bet they won't have my favorite. None of these fancy places ever have it." As Ernie viewed the menu, he made a point of giving me the play-by-play of the entrees he didn't want. "Veal Parmesan, no way. I don't eat veal. Lobster ravioli. What's wrong with good old meat ravioli?"

Finally, I asked, "If you could have anything you want, what would it be?"

The answer was fettuccine Alfredo. When the waiter was asked if the chef could make it, the answer was "yes." That's all it took for Ernie to get what he wanted. It was that simple. But Ernie admitted that it hadn't occurred to him to ask. He was so accustomed to not getting what he wanted that he had stopped believing it was possible. "Better to expect the worst than be disappointed" had become his mantra.

Ernie had plenty of stories and justifications for being unhappy, but he decided that he was willing to make a change. At any given moment, you have a choice. You can keep attracting what you don't want or you can choose to attain an outcome you do want. When you attract what you want, your energy level goes up. When you attract what you don't want, your energy is depleted. It's up to you whether you fill or drain your energy reservoir.

The process I share below is the same one I guided Ernie to complete so he could fill his energy reservoir and begin living the life he really wanted to live.

NEW POSSIBILITIES AND OUTCOMES

This exercise will help you to recognize and describe new possibilities and outcomes in your life.

Divide a sheet of paper into two vertical columns. In the left column, list the dissatisfactions in your life. In the right column, describe the new outcome you want for each dissatisfaction you've listed.

When you complete this exercise, you'll have a succinct list of the outcomes you most want to experience. By focusing on these outcomes, directly asking for what you want and making clear "yes" and "no" choices, you can create the life you want.

The best indication that this tool or any of the others described is working is for you to experience and witness the results yourself. You can deplete your life reservoir or enhance it. The love and energy you have for yourself expands in the ways in which you communicate and participate. It's up to you to decide.

About the Author

Carol Stringham

Carol leads individuals and groups to live more rewarding and successful lives by having them become conscious and clear about how they are communicating and participating in life. She is a professional speaker, teacher, therapist and personal life trainer. Her knowledge of and experience in personal and professional development, interpersonal communication, metaphysical philosophy, psychology and natural health combine to form the foundation for her courses and writings. She identifies and inspires people to develop skills that are critical to their success in relationships and in their business and professions.

Her laser vision and clarity help to pinpoint people's barriers so they can make choices that lead to more fulfilling lives.

Carol has studied and lived metaphysical principles for over 20 years and conducts weekend workshops to raise prosperity consciousness. She has been tenacious in her conducting of women's groups and studies on relationships so that women will live their passion and truth. She is a world traveler and has raised two sons with the wisdom and insights she has gleaned.

Carol and her husband, Peter Scott Stringham, created Grist Mill Mentors to encourage individuals, organizations and businesses to reach their highest potential. Grist Mill Mentors offers a variety of presentations, seminars, workshops and a monthly newsletter.

Grist Mill Mentors
SEMINARS & COACHING SERVICES

CAROL STRINGHAM

Carol offers a variety of training and coaching services that provide men and women with tools to awaken their inner power to manifest their desires. With her husband and partner Peter, she has been living and working on the site of a 1600s-era grist mill where she has been leading workshops and providing training services since 1991. Her offerings include:

Training: The use of specific tools that, if applied, will lead to a more abundant and prosperous life are taught in individual and group settings.

Coaching: One-on-one sessions are available to those wishing to have an ongoing coaching relationship.

Online classes and tele-seminars: Check her website for a listing of upcoming programs.

TRAININGS

The Abundance Workshop: The use of tools for living a more satisfied life is taught at this two-day workshop, inspiring new opportunities and life direction. Facilitated by Carol, she is one of only two certified facilitators to teach this workshop nationwide.

Seasons and Cycles of Prospering: Using a nine-year model created by master teacher Toni Stone, this-one day workshop is based on the four seasons. Discover where you are in your own life cycle, what it means, and what actions would be beneficial for the short term and the long term.

MONTHLY GROUP

Women's Group: Empowering conversations and exercises guide women toward living their full potential in their work and their relationships with others and themselves.

Grist Mill Mentors
P.O. Box 269
New Castle, NH 03854
603-433-5633
www.gristmillmentors.com

Here's what clients say about Carol:

"I express infinite gratitude to you for the ongoing gifts of learning and honest feedback toward my personal and spiritual growth. I keep returning to the 'well.'"

"Women's Group is a warm and challenging environment in which we can explore ourselves. You provide a compassionate mirror. I know that it isn't always easy for you to be as completely direct with people as your job requires, but you do it anyway because you know it is needed, and it is helpful."

Thank you for dedicating yourself to this work. It has helped me so much. I have really come out of my shell and started living more fully. You set a wonderful example of living a prosperous life."

"Thank you for inspiring me and supporting me to live a bigger life."

Chapter Three

Laying Your Soul Foundation

by Laura Murphy

A house built on sand isn't going to last. When we take the time to create a solid foundation physically, spiritually and mentally, we can create what we desire. If you have space for more joy, love, energy, could love your body more, haven't found your soul purpose, or know your purpose but aren't living it, this chapter is from my heart to yours.

If you're like many others, you might have read the books and been to the seminars, yet somehow you still don't seem to be manifesting the things you most desire. So, what's missing?

What's missing for most people is a solid foundation for manifestation. A house that looks great on the outside may have no substance underneath and therefore can crumble under even the slightest pressure. This is true for people, too. Are you one of those people who look like they have it all? Those people are like the beautiful house that any realtor would be happy to show: gorgeous banisters, sparkling chandelier, wide-plank hardwood floors—everything looks perfect. What the buyer doesn't know until a professional inspection is completed is that there is a huge crack in the foundation. Or you might be the type of person who has foundational cracks that are obvious and perhaps even easy to spot. No matter what your foundation looks like, this chapter will give you the tools for taking a close look and repairing any cracks or weaknesses you discover. In general, the bigger the gap between where you are and where you want to be, the bigger the crack in the foundation. A home built without a solid foundation eventually crumbles. If you've been repeating the same work over and over with no lasting results, you may have been building on a flimsy foundation.

The question you will be holding in your mind: "Is my foundation strong enough to create the life I desire?" By inspecting your foundation, you can see what areas are vulnerable and implement the missing structures of support. Shoring up your foundation will enable you to become the powerful master of manifestation you were born to be.

Let's start the foundation assessment by answering these questions. Please answer on a scale of 1-10, with 1 being the lowest rank and 10 meaning it couldn't possibly get any better.

1. How connected to and supported by source do you feel? (God, divine, nature, spirit, Allah, angels, higher power, your community, etc.)

2. How joy-filled is your life?

3. How much do you love your body?

4. Are your relationships based on honesty and total love? (full self-expression, trust, faith, fun, whole hearted acceptance, shared values and understanding.)

5. How satisfied are you in your community?

6. How much time do you spend in total alignment with your divine purpose?

7. How satisfied are you with the distance between your current reality and the life of your dreams?

8. How delighted are you with your financial circumstances?

Whether you have identified a solid foundation (10's), a rocky foundation (6-9's), or a crumbling pile of sand (<6's), there are steps you can take right now to get exactly where you want to go.

THE LOGISTICS OF YOUR FOUNDATION

You get to customize your foundation for the dream you're envisioning. Let's take a look at the physical world as our guide to the nonphysical.

Create a vision. To build a solid house, the first step is to create blueprints and obtain permits. For your manifestation, that's the equivalent of creating a clear, detailed vision of where you are headed. This is where you share what you're up to with your loved ones and invite them to share in the excitement of your goal. This enrolls people into the possibility of your dream and creates space for them to contribute to its manifestation. You can also invite them to share their visions with you. Perhaps every family member will want to create a vision board so you can display them together as you hold the space for each other's dreams and visions.

Prepare. In building your house, you need to know whether you're laying the foundation on clay, sand or rocky soil. It is unlikely that you would try to grow beautiful roses in soil of sand. You would clear the sand and spend some time creating the soil that will best nurture your new rosebushes. Allow yourself to be totally honest about the soil of your soul. What is beneath the surface? Is there rubbish that needs to be cleared from the building site before you lay the foundation? Are there past wounds or hurts that need to heal? Are there pressing health issues, fear or a need to feel supported? What are the stories, thoughts, patterns and beliefs that are in the way? Do you have addictions you need to address? Revealing the truth will allow you to answer the next critical question: "What support do I need to move forward in my full power, without being held back by the past?" Get clear. And clear the way for the next step.

Dig. This is when you dig out the area where the foundation will be laid. When you dig, you may need to enlist the support of experts who can help you to break through the obstacles you encounter. What support do you need? Is it a book, a coach, a therapist, a support group or a seminar? Once you identify what would support you, whether it's a therapist to heal past wounds or a coach to support you in a future-focused manner, implement that support structure now. This step is essential to allowing what will come next.

Lay your future grid. Now that you have a fresh template for creation, you can install all the things you need to have under your slab: electrical wiring, plumbing and drainage. In the spiritual sense, laying your future grid equates to creating structure in your life for strengthening your connection with divine spirit. Where will you meditate or get quiet each day? How much time will you spend? How will you stay accountable to make it an expectation just like your expectation that water will flow when you turn on the faucet? The water flows because the plumbing was properly installed. When we're quiet, when we allow our higher self to offer input, we can create a new foundation or fill in the cracks of our current one. So if you have four children and you think you will find time to meditate in the afternoon when they're playing or doing homework, you may want to look from a new perspective and see what could consistently and reliably work no matter what. Is it family meditation?

While the idea of family meditation may seem impossible, it's not as hard as it sounds. When I was an elementary-school teacher, we meditated every morning. At the beginning of the year, it lasted only 60 seconds, and we built up the time from there. If you make it playful and guide them, children are often much better at it than adults!

Set boundaries. This is pouring the concrete into the frame you have laid out for the foundation. I worked with a single mom with a hyperactive son. Once he knew how to tell time, she set a clear boundary for him. She used that time to connect to her breath, her spirit, her higher power. It was a time to ask for divine messages and listen for the answers. It was the time of day that was just for her to do what energized her for the day. From 7 to 7:30 a.m., Mommy was in meditation. That meant he was responsible for playing quietly or entertaining himself. He learned from experience how much more fun Mommy was after her meditation, so he honored that time (usually). Where in your life would better boundaries serve you?

Be flexible, not rigid. After laying plastic sheeting so that water doesn't seep up, we top it with a layer of sand so we're not rigid in our foundation. Even buildings are made to bend. Here, we go with the flow. Even though we need a solid foundation, we can't be rigid or we'll crack under stress. If we learn to be compassionate with ourselves and allow some flexibility, life's challenges don't stop us. Where can you infuse some flexibility into your spirit connection?

Bring the power. In a solid house foundation, there is a web of reinforcing steel. In your spiritual life, there is a super strong, non-bending support structure. Many of my clients find this strong support by joining a meditation group. When I'm in the mood for group meditation, I walk to the Chopra Center, where free silent meditations are offered during the week. For you, it may be joining an inspiring e-mail list that sends you an e-mail each day or joining a spiritual or religious community. Widen your web. Where might you be able to get more support to keep yourself in alignment with your vision?

Pour the concrete. For our physical foundation, this is when we pour the concrete into our well-planned and prepared space. In our spirit lives, this is where we practice. We meditate. We connect. We allow ourselves to be supported. We find ways to make it playful and do the work. This empowers us to be in action. Look to your structure of support. Surrender and allow.

MEDITATION CREATES A SOLID FOUNDATION

Meditation is a time to get quiet, turn your attention inward and listen. There are many styles and types of meditation. In my experience, the best type of meditation is the kind that works best for you. Experiment. Find what feels good. For those of you who are beginners, meditation can be approached just like physical fitness. If you've never run more than a few blocks, you probably wouldn't start by running a full mile, much less a marathon.

Your job is to identify your meditation starting point. Is it two minutes of silence in the morning? Is it mindful meditation as you walk on the beach or through a forest? Is it with a group of people? Is it allowing yourself to connect to source as you listen to uplifting music? Is it downloading a meditation application and being guided? Look into your heart, ask and trust the answers that come. Find a starting point that feels realistic and helpful. Play and experiment.

I worked with a man who drove himself crazy trying to do silent, still meditation. He signed up for a retreat and ended up leaving early feeling like a failure. He came home deflated and upset. A few weeks later, he related a story of walking through the woods. He lived in an area full of wildlife and talked about a specific hike he had taken. He shared how connected he felt to spirit, the visions he had of his future, and how he'd come home energized and excited. What he didn't see was that he had found his ideal way to connect to source. He liked moving meditation.

Interestingly, a few years later, he began to expand his practice. He was able to complete the 10-day Vipassana retreat because he had honored his starting point years earlier.

If you're a veteran in the realm of meditation, you may want to look at whether it's time for a change. Just like doing the same workout every day can stop producing the same results, this is often the case with a meditation practice that has gotten stale. How can you expand your learning and your practice to grow? Is it a new teacher, a new style of meditation or expanding the time you spend silently each day? How can you integrate change into your meditation practice today to get a boost in your connection?

Keep in mind that your physical, spiritual and mental well-being determine the strength and stability of your foundation. We've all experienced the effects of being undernourished or sleep-deprived. We may have made a big mistake at work, locked ourselves out of the house or even had a life-changing accident. Physical well-being is just as important as spiritual well-being. Both are vital for building the life you desire.

I can't tell you how many times I've gotten on the phone with clients who just can't understand why they aren't manifesting or producing results when they are working so hard. A client I'll call Sally had a full-time job, two kids and had just started her own business on the side. She was committed to perform-ing well at work, being there for her kids and making a go of her business. Who had time to sleep enough or eat well, let alone meditate?

Despite some initial resistance, Sally was willing to look at her well-being as an access point to the life she wanted. For two months, she took on her well-being like her life depended on it. She made a list of actions that would support her, ranging from taking a hot bath to daily meditation to dancing with her kids. She created goals each week that specified the actions she would take.

Not surprisingly, things started shifting for Sally. She started enjoying more time with her kids and she came up with brilliant ideas for cutting back her hours at work without sacrificing quality, which, in turn, gave her more time to devote to her business. Sally created all this by focusing on her health and her connection to spirit.

THE 60-DAY WELL-BEING CHALLENGE

I dare you to take the 60-day well-being challenge. Here are the steps:

1. Make a list of 10 things that would support your well-being. They can be physical, spiritual or emotional. Create variety and really look inward for what would most serve you daily. Examples my clients have created include singing, taking a multivitamin, drinking 10 glasses of water, walking in nature, sleeping at least eight hours, flossing, meditating, dancing, writing, drawing, surfing and pulling oracle cards.

2. Invite a buddy to play the game with you. Hold each other accountable each week.

3. Create a tracker and keep it simple. Post it where you can see it every day, and mark which of the things you did.

4. Reward yourself each week when you hit your goal.

5. Notice how you feel.

WHAT'S NEXT?

Now that you have the tools, you're ready to honor your physical well-being as an access point to your nonphysical well-being. Please take a few minutes to get clear by writing your answers to the following questions:

1. What is the current status of your foundation for the life of your dreams? Does it need some updating or a total overhaul?

2. What support do you need to clear the space to lay a new foundation?

3. Have you designed a clear vision for your future? If not, please take 15 minutes to visualize your life 10 years from now. Envision the life you would love to be living. Imagine how it feels, notice what you're doing and who you're with, and write it all down. Yep, right now. Just 15 minutes. The odds that you'll get what you want are much better if you see it and ask clearly!

4. Make a list of 20 things that will support you physically, mentally, emotionally and spiritually if you do them consistently. Choose 10 for this week and then start your weekly tracking. This can be a simple checklist, an Excel spreadsheet or a tracker in columns where you give yourself gold stars for each one you complete every day.

5. Create your space for connecting to source. Choose whether it's an altar, a comfy chair in your backyard or your living-room floor. Where will you go when it's time to connect?

6. If you let yourself be totally honest, what can you foresee that might get in the way of creating the life of your dreams? What support do you need to ensure that the barriers you perceive won't stop you? If you know you need someone to work on this with you, find a coach who believes in the life of your dreams and will help you to do what's necessary to build it.

The time is now. The truth is, you are worth it. Yes, building or redesigning a foundation takes time. But when you walk into that new home of your dream life, won't it be worth it? If you're like most human beings, there might still be that little voice (that one that isn't a fan of change or growth) that says, "It's too hard," "It will take too long," "It will cost too much money," or, "I already tried that."

The truth is, you can listen to that voice and keep going the way you've been going, or you can take a single step today. A single step right now that will move you forward in laying your soul foundation. If you'd like a partner in that journey, I'm here to support you, and you can e-mail me right now (laura@ lauramurphy.net). If you feel moved to get a group together, go for it. Just one day at a time, one step at a time. You are worth it. Imagine what gifts the universe will receive when you allow yourself to step into your greatness. Imagine our planet when all people step into their greatness. It gives me chills just thinking about it!

About the Author

Laura Murphy

Laura Murphy loves the process of transformation and being a ripple in the pond of growth, discovery and joy. She is presence, power, radiance, love, connection. Her titles include certified life coach, speaker, author, mentor coach and workshop facilitator. She is trained in Reiki, is a former elementary-school teacher, has degrees in psychology and metaphysics, and is passionate about transformation on our planet.

When Laura isn't working, you'll often find her surfing, which is one of her favorite ways to connect to spirit and go with the flow. She also loves to dance, sing and spend time enjoying the wonders of nature.

Because Laura is committed to transformation on the planet, she continually looks to where she might be able to be of service. Whether it's a college student wanting to step into his greatness and new levels of maturity, a successful professional who is yearning for more balance with her family, or a business executive wanting to increase his effectiveness at work, Laura loves to play with people who are ready to take ownership of their lives and live their dreams.

She is known for asking tough questions, holding her clients in love and relating to them as the superheroes they really are. "What layers need to come off to expose this person's superhero nature?" is a question that arises regularly for her.

She is president and founder of Laura Murphy Coaching. She is also an affiliate coach with Accomplishment Coaching, one of the most elite coach-training programs in the world. She loves supporting new coaches as they deepen their roots while learning to fly.

Laura Murphy Coaching

Stepping into my life's purpose has been an extraordinary process. I knew I wanted to contribute to society, and no matter what job I did, I always seemed to end up coaching people on what was going on in their lives. As a volleyball coach, I never did have a championship team, but our players were in touch with their hearts and got support for life issues such as divorce, eating disorders and relationships. As a teacher, I often was more concerned with a child's life development than his or her multiplication tables. In the nonprofit world, whether I was working with gay youths or people living with HIV, I always seemed to sneak coaching into whatever I was doing.

It took many years of having "life coach" as a goal before I was ready to take the plunge. Perhaps you can identify in some way. Maybe your job doesn't speak to your spirit but you don't think changing is possible, especially if you have something very adult like a mortgage and children! You might think you're too old, or it's just too late.

Well, there is hope. I have had the opportunity to make the transition myself and support many others in their own unique life journeys. I meet my clients wherever they are in their process of discovery. My coaching has no agenda other than to support you to create the breakthroughs and shifts you desire. As we work on those goals, I'll support you to get clear on who you really are. Some people call this "essence," and I often joke that it's you embracing your closeted superhero. Whatever you want to call it, our work is to create lasting shifts that allow you to uncover the true "you" that is full of heart, passion and possibility to shine.

You may already know exactly what is in the way, or you may not have any idea. I often refer to myself as a three-way mirror. I am able to have a different vantage point from which to see things you may not be able to see and support you to embrace your life from a new, more powerful place.

Through my intuition, passionate heart and your guidance, we can work together to support you in creating and manifesting the life of your dreams. To be clear, I don't mean the small goals or dreams you're pretty sure you'd accomplish on your own. I mean the big, amazing, you'd–jump-up-and-down-if-you-did-that dreams.

So whatever that is, I'd love to support you. Feel free to e-mail and share what you're up to. I'd love to be your partner as you step fully into the truth of who you are, release that which no longer serves you, and support you as you build your castle on the foundation for the life of your dreams!

www.lauramurphy.net

CHAPTER FOUR

Optimal Health: It's not what you think or do; it's who you become

by Dr. Bruce Hoffman

A new patient, whom I'll call Jane, recently came in to see me with symptoms of crippling fatigue, anxiety, depression and body pain that had been present for three years. She said the symptoms had started when she was 44 and she had seen many medical doctors and naturopaths, been to the Mayo Clinic and had numerous blood tests and special investigations. The resulting diagnosis: atypical depression. This is the catchall of the medical profession when no discernible causative factor or factors can be ascertained.

Although further tests did reveal significant biochemical imbalances, what was most revealing to me was her obvious dissatisfaction with her life, her anger toward her mother and a generalized sense of boredom. "I am my father's daughter," she said through clenched teeth. "I despise my mother." Later, she explained, "I'm an engineer like my dad, but I haven't worked for 12 years, because I wanted to stay home and bring up my daughter."

Jane, like many people, was primarily interested in eliminating, or at least managing, her symptoms. This is true for many new patients until I teach them the 7 Stages of Health and Transformation™, which I designed to assist in diagnosing and treating complex presentations that defy traditional explanation. (For a detailed explanation, visit www.hoffmancentre.com.) Each stage looks at a different aspect of the individual so that the entire human being is assessed and healing methods can be focused on the true causes of illness. Once Jane increased her understanding of optimal health, she said she wanted more than to simply get rid of her symptoms. She wanted to achieve a positive state of well-being. She wanted to find meaning in her life and enjoy herself and her family. Now Jane was being motivated by an aspiration toward something more than an absence of symptoms: an expanded sense of well-being and wholeness. With this goal in mind, she became fully engaged in a deeper relationship with herself, self-healing, her loved ones and the planet as a whole. Her three-year inquiry into her symptoms had produced a lot of information about the signs and symptoms of disease, but now she was open to learning about the signs and symptoms of health. This expanded paradigm includes a deep sense of inner vitality, integration and self-knowing and entails creating and sustaining healthy relationships and having a sense of meaning and purpose in life. It's important to note that many people are not interested in pursuing this level of health, so, as a physician, one of my first responsibilities is to determine and clarify each patient's goals for health and respond accordingly.

Since Jane was revealing a desire to be whole, her journey would be quite different from that of a patient who is merely seeking relief of symptoms. As Carl Jung observed, "As far as we can discern, the sole purpose of human existence is to kindle a light in the darkness of mere being." To me, this means leading a life of inspired creativity rather than an ordinary existence of mere tolerance against a backdrop of the mundane.

For many people, this desire to shine with their true essence emerges around the midpoint of their lives. Sometimes it's a conflict with a midlife transition that brings them into the office. Their symptoms often arise as a result of a discrepancy between what their ego wants (first-half-of-life endeavors) and what their deepest, unconscious self desires (the aspirations of the second half of life). What our deepest self or soul wants is often hidden from our conscious view, clouded by the busyness and adaptive strategies of the first half of life's innumerable and overwhelming demands and by our vague value systems, which are not yet fully developed. Therefore, the task of a healer working at this level is to assist in helping patients identify the blocking factors preventing them from achieving what their soul is seeking and what their minds are trying to keep hidden. Symptoms are often the entry point in this inquiry.

What drives us in the first half of life are often the wishes and wants of authority figures, as well as the innate selfish Darwinian gene that wishes to perpetuate the species by mating with the most suitable partner from whatever gene pool available. Thus, with the help of a hormone-drenched physiology, we develop a strong sense of a personal ego-driven self. We strive to achieve the highest standards that our gene pool can

achieve. We educate ourselves, fall in love, marry, create financial security and buy the most suitable home so as to provide
safety for our offspring. We feel accomplished upon achieving
some modicum of success in these areas. But in the process, we
push aside the whisperings and nuances of a deeper core self,
and our adaptive personas do a fabulous job of hiding that core
self from view. Symptoms are often the first message from our
core self that not all is well in our adaptive situation. This was
the case with Jane.

It is usually in the second half of life that the first whisperings of our hidden potentials and possibilities emerge. We are
often plagued by lingering doubts and questions such as "Is
this all there is?" "Is this what I really want?" "Am I fulfilling my true potential?" "Is this partner really aligned with my
values?" "Does my partner see who I really am?" and "Should I
be doing something else with my life?"

It is at this exact interface between what the ego has strived to
achieve and what the soul really wants that symptoms appear,
as if to draw us into a deeper inquiry with ourselves. It has been
my observation that symptoms at this level serve as feedback
from our core self, drawing our attention to that which is most
neglected within us and which needs our conscious attention.

At this level, when one is ill or symptomatic, no amount of
goal setting or life-purpose strategies will fulfill the deeper
drives that are asking for attention. Often, the continued pur-
suit of goals and life-purpose strategies of the ego-based first
half of life are the very reason for a lingering sense of malaise.
No mental strategies, no goal setting and no mission statements will succeed when we find ourselves in this position. On

the contrary, they will make us sicker, driving us further from the very aspect of ourselves that's calling for attention.

Most often, the answer to the patient's malaise will surface only after a much deeper inquiry and a much deeper surrender are made, a surrender to his or her own unconscious and to a larger wisdom than the ego-based mind. At this level of healing, one has to listen to the many different ways that the psyche expresses itself in its desire to unify all its components.

Actively listening to our bodies is one profound tool we can use to seek information outside our rational ego-based mindset. Dreams are spontaneous messages from the unconscious, suggesting symbolic ways of seeing issues we cannot see or understand with our conscious, ego minds. Synchronicities—when an event in the outer world coincides meaningfully with a psychological state of mind—may also provide us with clues to the directions our soul may want to take.

Sometimes symptoms or illness at this level may also arise from an issue within a family system, some entanglement or secret that has never been consciously exposed. Unresolved traumas can affect family members for multiple generations. Family Constellation therapy can cover the unconscious bonds and loyalties that underlie many physical and emotional symptoms. It has been my observation that very often the inner healer cannot be accessed if the client isn't fully aligned with his or her birth mother or father.

When my patient Jane said, "I despise my mother," it was a dead giveaway that she didn't have access to her full life force and inner healer. No amount of nutrition, bodywork or depth psychology can heal someone in this situation. Jane had to turn inward and uncover the inner, unconscious entanglements that were hidden from her conscious view.

In Jane's case, after a long dialogue investigating her family dynamics, it was clear that her rejection of her mother and her overidentification with her father had led to an imbalance in her psyche between the masculine and feminine lineages. It has been observed in family-system dynamics that the energy we take from our mothers provides us with our day-to-day relational energy, nurtures us and gives us life; fathers' energy organizes and provides a context for the unfolding of our life force. For a very long time, Jane had been under the influence of her father's desires, negated her mother's character and positive influence and subjugated her own deeper, soul-based desires to the point of total silence. It's often seen that people experiencing fatigue are living not according to their own inner value systems but according to those of outer authority figures that have been unconsciously adopted as one's own, in this case those of Jane's father.

It took many months of her listening intensely to the symptoms of her body, paying attention to her dreams, asking her body for guidance and turning to her healer within before she could see her way clear to her true, creative self's path. And her symptoms escalated all the while. Although much work was done optimizing her adrenal function, treating her Epstein-Barr virus infection, balancing glutathione levels and tweaking her hormones—treatment at the outer, physical level—it wasn't until she turned inward that the healing occurred. When she saw her symptoms, not as some curse to be eradicated but as harbingers, whisperings of the need for a deeper inquiry, she did what it took to begin her healing journey, her return to wholeness.

When she faced the deeper issues that were asking to be revealed, she realized that being a wife and a mother was only a fraction of her true vocation. She saw that what she had proudly worn as a badge of honor—being Daddy's little girl—was a trap from which she had to escape. She realized that she was not living her authentic values but those of her father. As she softened her rejecting stance toward her mother, accepting and seeing her clearly for the first time, and as she turned inward, Jane's inner healer was activated. She learned to trust her own body and instincts for the first time. She had resisted this inward movement for years and seen countless excellent physicians and healers to get the latest outer remedies, all to no avail. But once she recognized her symptoms as messages from her soul and learned how to pay attention, her healing was dramatic.

For true healing to occur, we must expand our lens of inquiry to identify the multilayered blocking factors hindering our sense of wellness and self-fulfillment and determine where these experiences are occurring in our lives. Furthermore, we must listen to our symptoms and our bodies to see if they provide any information that will assist us in integrating those neglected parts of ourselves that are hidden from our conscious, rational points of view. The following exercise will help you to begin to do this.

CREATIVE IMAGERY: LISTENING TO YOUR CELLS

1. Come into contact with yourself and taste your own presence. Welcome and cherish your own presence in this world.

2. Breathe in, breathe out.

3. Let the physical tensions go and relax the mental tensions.

4. Place your attention in your heart, your soul.

5. Let your attention go to the place in you that has a lot of pain or symptoms. It can be a mental place or a physical place, a muscle or an organ.

6. Approach this area with respect, tenderness and care. Talk to this area. You are talking to these cells in a time of difficulty. Memories may arise.

7. Say, "I am here now to listen to you." Let whatever comes from that place speak to you.

8. Allow the messages of the cells to come to you. These cells represent the strength of life trying to talk to you and connect with you. This attitude of listening and respect, without discussion, is already healing you.

9. Now that your cells or your symptoms finally have your attention, say to this area or set of symptoms, "You don't need to keep showing up in this way. You now have my attention."

10. With the same care and respect, begin to transform. Imagine your stem cells coming from your shoulder

blade or hipbone, where your bone marrow is active, and flooding the tissue that's in need of healing.

11. Imagine your stem cells flowing through to the place where you're suffering. Imagine them dancing and producing color and light.

12. Let this dance take part in all of your cells and in your entire psyche, producing an experience of healing. Soon all your body is light and warm. Rejoice in the health that these stem cells bring.

13. Imagine yourself becoming luminous from this sensation, nourishing yourself and everybody around you.

14. Imagine what you will do with yourself once your health is restored. Where will you go to nourish your health, and what creative choices will you make?

15. Imagine yourself doing things you like, things that give you an intensified love of life.

16. When you're ready, open your eyes and make a note of what you experienced, what you saw and what new image or images have arisen for you.

When we approach healing through a truly holistic model, it becomes a profound, courageous, spiritual act of coming to wholeness, where the body is relatively healthy, the emotions are stable and the mind is clear and focused. Spiritually, our destiny is clear and yet we remain humbled to an intelligence that's greater than ourselves but from which we derive daily guidance and sustenance and to which we give thanks. Alternatively, it may mean that the deepest essence of the individual is in an integrated or individuated, whole place in spite of the body's having symptoms or a disease. They are identified with that which is timeless within them. The awareness is that they are not physical machines that have learned how to think. They are not, as Deepak Chopra likes to say, "skin-encapsulated egos squeezed into the volume of a body in the span of a lifetime." They are not these constricted, isolated individual entities that Western medicine may want us to believe they are. At their core, they are identified with that which is defined as an unbounded, infinite, eternal, ever-present witnessing awareness. They are consciously aware of being a network of energy and intelligence inextricably interwoven into the web of life.

REACHING FOR ABSOLUTE HEALTH

Some people choose to seek a level of health that is even beyond wholeness, a level that might be called absolute health. They want to heal their physical bodies so they can live out their lives in a state of maximum potential and in the fulfillment of love and purpose and feel the joy, wisdom and compassion in their lives more fully.

We achieve this not by medicating symptoms but by using them as feedback mechanisms to let us know where we need to become more conscious. We learn to "lean into the sharp points of our lives", as Pema Chodron has said. With this knowledge, we don't retreat from the world—we consciously engage with the world as we start to wake up to the wonder of our existence.

We start to address the questions raised by the poet Mary Oliver: "What are you going to do with this one wild precious life?" This heartfelt recognition of the preciousness of human life is the second-most essential step on the path to integral health. The first is to recognize that our true nature is more than our bodies, our emotions, our minds and our possessions and that there is an intelligence guiding us that we can turn to and trust. We start to celebrate in the miracle and sacredness of our human existence.

Einstein said there are only two ways to live your life. One is "as if nothing is a miracle," and the second is "as if everything is a miracle." The word *miracle* comes from the word *mirari*, which means "to wonder," "to smile," "to break into joy" and "to release."

Once we awaken to the preciousness of our lives, we enjoy a level of wholeness and vitality that is beyond our physical body and mortal mind. We connect with our true self, which is nonlocal, outside of space/time, immortal, eternal and incapable of death.

REFERENCES:

1. Elliot Dacher. *Integral Health.*

2. Carl Jung. *Memories, Dreams and Reflections.*

3. David Simon. Keynote address at Ayurvedic conference. Berkeley.

4. Pema Chodron. *When Things Fall Apart.*

5. Guy Corneau. Lecture, Jung Society, 2012.

6. James Hollis. *The Middle Passage.*

ABOUT THE AUTHOR

Dr. Bruce Hoffman

Dr. Bruce Hoffman, a medical doctor and impassioned healer, is a key contributor to the revolution in conventional medicine. He earned his medical degree from the University of Cape Town, South Africa, in 1981 and moved to Canada in 1985. Dr. Hoffman received his board certification and fellowship in anti-aging, rejuvenative and functional medicine in 2009 and his MSc in nutrition and metabolic medicine in 2012.

Dr. Hoffman has studied many of the major disciplines in the broad scope of integrative medicine, including anti-aging medicine, bioidentical hormone replacement therapy, German biological medicine, homotoxicology, functional medicine, energy psychology, Ayurvedic and Chinese medicine, Family Constellation therapy and Jungian psychology. In addition to his clinical training, Dr. Hoffman has studied with leading mind-body and spiritual healers, including Deepak Chopra, Dr. John Demartini, Paul Lowe, Osho, Ramesh Balsekar and Jon Kabat-Zinn.

As medical director of the Hoffman Centre for Integrative Medicine, Dr. Hoffman leads the field of integrative medicine and the emerging field of mind/body health, spirituality and medicine in Canada. His groundbreaking 7 Stages to Health and Transformation™ model offers an inspiring vision of health, healing and self-actualization.

With the 7 Stages to Health and Transformation™ model, Dr. Hoffman has created a new curriculum for integrative medicine. It is a broadly defined system of medicine that combines traditional medicine with proven and effective complementary/alternative therapies at all levels of a person's experience. This is concisely defined as whole-person healing.

It is one of the first working models in integrative medicine to masterfully incorporate the environment, body, energy, emotions, mind, soul and spirit into a single system of healing and to systemically organize many of the diagnostic and therapeutic options accordingly.

Hoffman Centre
FOR INTEGRATIVE MEDICINE

Dr. Bruce Hoffman, MSc, MBChB, FAARFM
1133 17th Avenue NW, Calgary, AB T2M 0P7
Telephone: (403) 206-2333
Facsimile: (403) 206-2334
info@hoffmancentre.com
www.hoffmancentre.com

AREAS OF CONSULTING EXPERTISE:

- Chronic Illness – cancer, autoimmune, neurological, chronic fatigue/fibromyalgia, autism, Lyme disease

- Anti-Aging & Bioidentical Hormone Therapy

- Functional Medicine

- Family Constellation Therapy

- Demartini Method

BOOKS

- 7 Stages to Health & Transformation™ Workbook and PowerPoint Presentation

- Thank God I... "Thank God I Lost My Home" chapter

- North America's Top Doctors Share Secrets to Anti-Aging & Wellness – Chapter 5, "Male Menopause"

CDs & DVDs

- 7 Stages to Health & Transformation – CD

- Healing Consciousness, with John Demartini – DVD

- Relationships – An Ayurvedic Approach – CD

- Tragedy – The Divine Order – CD

- Healing and the Mind Body Connection, with John Demartini – CD & DVD

- ADHD & Autism, with John Demartini – DVD

CHAPTER FIVE

Happiness Attracts Success

by Conrad Toner

About 30 years ago, while I was still actively farming, the international organization CUSO (Canadian University Students Overseas) invited me to travel to Nicaragua shortly after a bitter civil war had ended there. One of the consequences of the devastation caused by that war was that the country was out of seed potatoes, so a number of Canadian farmers shipped seed there and got them planting again. I was asked to go along to help oversee the project.

At one of those co-ops, I met a young man who had lost both his legs in that horrendous conflict. He was sitting contentedly on the doorstep of his modest home as I approached him. Since most of the country's medical facilities had been destroyed, I was surprised that he had survived such a major injury. But I was even more surprised, given his present lot in life, that he seemed so serene with his current circumstances.

His explanations were astounding.

He had survived the war, he told me, not so much because of any minimal medical care he had received but because he believed he still had a purpose in life. His goal, he went on to explain, was "to free my children's children." And to accomplish that, given the meager resources available, he in effect had to heal himself.

I've never forgotten that brave man's words. How powerful they are! Meeting and speaking with him was a great privilege, one of the highlights of that trip.

Now, since that time, I've been to many other countries where I continue to encounter hundreds of individuals with similar remarkable stories. These are, in every other way, rather "ordinary" people, yet somehow they are able to find happiness despite living in some of the poorest, most miserable conditions known to man.

In contrast, I've met others who have access to wealth and resources that most can only dream about, and yet I've been amazed to learn that many of them often find it hard to experience much real pleasure. Though these unfortunate souls may have every modern comfort and convenience, life is frequently overwhelming, little more than one daily struggle after another.

For a long time, I couldn't figure it all out. Why is it that certain people can find happiness even though the odds are stacked against them while others, who seem to have all the "advantages," can't even begin to enjoy what they have?

It does seem strange, doesn't it? And perhaps even a little unfair. That is, until you consider the Law of Attraction.

The Law of Attraction teaches us that happiness attracts success. It also holds that all of us have within ourselves everything we need to create that happiness. This realization—that we ourselves can actually create our own reality—ushers in a new way of thinking and living.

My friend in Nicaragua somehow already knew this instinctively by the time I met him. Meanwhile, it took me years and years to catch on. Nevertheless, we both learned in our own way that no matter what life throws at us, we are still able to go on and find pleasure and peace of mind. By consciously controlling our thoughts, we are able to decide who and what we want to become. In fact, that greater awareness and consciousness is exactly what gives us that power.

Now, this is hardly a new or revolutionary concept, to be sure. In his marvelous book *The Power of Positive Thinking*, Norman Vincent Peale said just about the same thing more than 50 years ago when he wrote, "Happiness doesn't depend on who you are or what you have. It depends solely on what you think." And we can go back much further than that. In the Bible, for example, Luke 17:21 reads, "The kingdom of God is within you." Personally, I have no trouble equating "the kingdom of God" with "happiness." So that passage, in my estimation, sounds no different from what Dr. Peale has to say.

Then, too, I remember my own mother telling us children over and over, "No one else can make you happy." With a mother like that, perhaps I was primed from an early age to believe that we are responsible for our own lives and that we can and must create our own happiness. One message I wish to leave with you today is that you, too, are able to create your own happiness. Moreover, you can begin to take charge right now because not only do you have access to that same kind of power but, no doubt, you're already using it.

Consciously or not, you already make such decisions. They're the ones about how you spend each moment of your day. As they accumulate, they eventually sum up who and what you want to be. Now, although I believe that controlling your thoughts consciously is exactly what can give you control over your life, the trouble is that most of us charge through life without giving these decisions a whole lot of deliberation. And that's where we get into difficulty. So if your life is ever going to change, it's crucial that a new thought pattern be developed, starting now, with "top-of-the-mind" awareness of what's actually going on inside your head.

If you can do that, I guarantee you a new and happier life. Think about it. Aren't the thoughts you have today pretty much just like the ones you had yesterday, the day before, a year ago or even five years ago? It's almost as if we sleepwalk or put ourselves on "autopilot" most of the time.

It's that perception of your life, one formed without any overall plan, that has created your current situation. But by using top-of-the-mind decisions going forward rather than leaving your autopilot in control, you can go after your dreams with more certainty. And the more certainty you gain, the more you will attract the things you need to move your life into higher gear. Before long, everything else will begin to fall into place because when you feel good about what you're doing, the right people come along or the right book falls into your hands and your thinking becomes crystal clear. Better yet, you become a magnet for more happiness. At that point, you'll even find yourself letting go of any negative emotions you may still be holding on to and you'll begin to tell yourself a happier story.

And our purpose in life, no matter how you phrase it, is to be happy. That's it. That's all. The secret is to pursue what makes you truly happy. That's why it is so important to identify your life purpose. It's what sets happy people apart from others.

Think again about that young Nicaraguan. He illustrates this so well. His purpose—to free his children's' children—allowed him to overcome incredible obstacles and find serenity. When we know what our purpose is, we can easily make choices that support that purpose.

JUST FOR TODAY

This is a wonderful way to begin each day.

1. For the next five minutes, ground yourself by concentrating only on your breathing.

2. Inhale for eight seconds and exhale for eight seconds. Repeat.

3. Let go of all other thoughts.

4. Let go of all judgment, remembering that your purpose today is just to be happy.

5. Allow divine order to take charge of your life just for this one day.

During the day, if something disturbs you, sit down for a minute and take a few deep breaths, ground yourself again and remind yourself that just for today you have chosen harmony, success, prosperity and abundance.

CREATING OUR OWN HAPPINESS

"Those who speak most of prosperity have it, and those who speak most of sickness or poverty have it. It is The Law. It can be no other way."
– Abraham, a group of entities "interpreted" by Esther Hicks

Earlier, I mentioned that we already have what we need to create our own happiness. I truly believe that. We do have that power and ability. And, I even make the process sound rather simple, don't I?

So, now you're probably wondering, "Well, if things really are that simple, why don't more people just go ahead and do it? What am I missing? What's holding everybody back?

Look around. There are lots of "ordinary" people in your life who do, in fact, lead extraordinarily happy lives. It's far more common than we believe. Let's not lose sight of that important fact. Nevertheless, such questions persist and deserve a more complete answer which I'll now propose.

To begin, I think people find it hard to see the truth of these ideas precisely because they are so simple. Perhaps because nearly everything else in their lives appears to be complicated, they figure that achieving happiness, too, must be so. And if something appears to be too complex, why bother? It's very easy to give up when you think that way, isn't it? Then there are people who seem to like the spot where they currently find themselves, no matter how uncomfortable it is. Once you decide you want to be happy, you have to give up all the whining and complaining and replace it with a determination to learn how to be happy. That, also, can seem overwhelming and undoubtedly holds many people back.

What, then, are they missing? Take another look around. Not only do you see "ordinary" people leading extraordinarily happy lives, but you also see others who are *never* happy. Some of them seem to be nasty and ungrateful all the time. Usually, the only people who will stand by them are others who are equally nasty and ungrateful. You know who I mean, don't you? We try to avoid such people because they tend to see a world in chaos, a place in which almost nothing is certain. These unhappy people can include some of your own friends and relatives, and they can lead you astray. You see, with such a negative outlook, their perception of life becomes fear-based rather than hopeful. They eventually end up surrounded by like-minded people. To live your life in fear, to rarely if ever know true pleasure and contentment—who would choose a life like that? Still, just as there are those who can find happiness in spite of difficulties, there are those who live their entire lives in fear.

Does it ever surprise you, then, when one of these mean-spirited people experiences a misfortune such as a business failure or a heart attack? Probably not. Nor, for that matter, are we amazed when a disgruntled kid in the neighborhood ends up throwing a rock through his or her window. Most of us expect them to get their just desserts sooner or later. "What goes around comes around," is the way we often put it.

So, that's the rest of my answer to "What's holding everybody back?" Just as the Law of Attraction states, it seems that those who complain about how difficult life is seem to "attract" more things into their life that make it so.

At this point, I have to ask: If we can easily believe that nasty, mean-spirited people will inevitably make things harder for themselves and bring about many of their own difficulties, shouldn't it naturally follow that the reverse process is equally true? Don't others just naturally gravitate toward people who are pleasant and focused on the positive aspects of life? Wouldn't you say that those people usually have an easier time of it? The ones who are truly at peace with themselves do, in fact, end up being surrounded by like-minded friends. In addition, they have the distinct advantage of being able to replace negative, hurtful or unproductive thoughts and vibrations with positive ones, day after day, all day long.

That's easier said than done, I know. But a friend of mine is almost there. He has a very successful business, and he really loves his work. Consequently, he is totally focused on improving the business—so much so that it has taken over all other aspects of his life. His business, then, has become what he values the most. His health and other aspects of life, unfortunately, hold less value at present. Now, as he ages, he has become angry and resentful about the way he feels about his health and those other matters. He talks about all that but is continually looking for quick fixes.

This underscores why we must put so much emphasis on balance. You see, whatever you focus on or value the most is exactly what you get more of. However, if there is too much focus in one area of your life, the other areas may suffer, as my businessman friend is finding out. He eventually will regain a balance in his life, I'm sure, and at that point, both his business and his personal life will benefit.

If you haven't yet noticed the truth of these statements or are still having a bit of trouble coming to grips with the whole idea, take note from here on out as you speak with your friends and relatives. You'll be blown away by what you'll hear now. People tell it the way it is without even realizing it.

You can run your own little experiment. Just listen closely as they speak. You'll hear comments like "I'm broke," "I can't afford that," "I can never find a job," "I'm always sick," "I hate my work" and "I'm not athletically inclined." What do you think is going to happen to those who say such things? By now, you should be able to figure out my answer.

It's relatively easy to see and believe that difficult people bring a lot of their troubles upon themselves. But for some reason, it's not so easy to see and believe that a similar process is also at work in our own lives. We ourselves don't fall into such traps or surround ourselves with negative people, do we? And we don't say things like "I can't afford that" or "I hate my work," do we?

Or …do we?

The truth is, most of us do. Now, we don't usually struggle with these issues to the point of becoming totally paralyzed. For the most part, we do experience some joy on a daily basis and are able to accomplish some good things from day to day, but we don't operate anywhere near what our true abilities would allow if unleashed.

So take notice of how you think. Notice how you talk. Notice the things you're saying to yourself and others. As Abraham said, "Those who speak most of prosperity have it, and those who speak most of sickness or poverty have it. It is The Law. It can be no other way." Dr. John Demartini also picks up on this concept when he writes, "What you think about and thank about you bring about."

Our minds are highly sophisticated and seem to be designed so that we find whatever we are looking for. Just as you can choose to be happy, you can also choose to struggle less and enjoy more. Begin by replacing your current way of thinking with the understanding that you are a powerful magnet and every word and thought attracts more of its own kind.

It's not unusual for my new clients to insist that they can't help how they feel. The myth that we are victims to our emotions has become so prevalent that people have begun to accept it as truth without even questioning it. But I'm here to tell you that it's nonsense. Our emotions stem from our perceptions and beliefs. And those perceptions and beliefs tend to change as we expand our knowledge and understanding and gain more life experience. Our perceptions can also change from day to day, depending on the circumstances. For example, when I was farming, if the crops needed water, I was glad when it rained. If we'd been getting too much rain, the thought of more rain could be upsetting, but only if I allowed my emotions to run away with me. You see, rain is just rain. It isn't good and it isn't bad. It was only my perception of rain that was good or bad.

For many, many years, I allowed my perceptions to dictate my emotions. Those times were an emotional roller coaster for me. Only in the past few years have I taken my mother's advice and chosen to be happy. Once I understood the wisdom of her advice, I was able to create joy in life no matter what was happening around me. I learned to be happy when it rained and happy when it didn't. If there's one thing I know for certain, it's that each one of us has plenty that we can be grateful for and happy about this very minute. So why wait?

Take five minutes right now to list the blessings in your life. Take a tour of your life and notice all the people and circumstances you appreciate. Continue making your list until you can feel your heart open. This warm, lighthearted feeling is true happiness. The more you focus on creating this feeling in your heart, the happier you will be and the more successful you will become.

About the Author

Conrad Toner

Conrad's clients and workshop participants experience "aha!" moments and use words like *passionate, motivating* and *insightful* when describing their time with him.

Conrad is a firm believer that success is a conscious choice. He's dedicated to helping his clients break through the limiting beliefs that keep them from living a life filled with love, peace and joy.

Conrad's life experience, education and training set him apart as a life coach, and it shows when he delivers his workshops, group coaching and personal one-on-one coaching. His clients come from all walks of life, but the common trait they share is a desire to have a life coach who is authentic, a listener and has the training and experience to help them move forward in the fastest way possible.

A graduate of the University of New Brunswick with a degree in interdisciplinary leadership philosophy, Conrad is also a consultant certified by the esteemed coaching organization 6 Advisors™ Academy. He is a graduate of the Advanced Agricultural Leadership Program and the Canadian Agriculture Leadership for Life Program and a Law of Attraction facilitator and trainer certified by Michael Losier.

Conrad has attained Level 3 in Reiki, a Japanese technique for stress reduction and relaxation that promotes healing. He is also certified in Level 3 Qigong, a traditional healing method that reduces stress.

A successful farmer for more than 30 years, Conrad has served as a global-justice participant delivering farm-related programs. He has lived, worked and learned alongside community leaders in Ethiopia, Bhutan, Mexico, Nicaragua and several South American countries.

Conrad and his wife, Linda, live in Grand Falls, New Brunswick. They have four adult children. Conrad enjoys golf, hockey, cross-country skiing and running. For leisure he reads, listens to music and meditates.

Conrad Toner Coaching

Controlling Thoughts Consciously

Office: 506-473-1785. Mobile: 506-475-9673
E-mail: coach@conradtoner.com
www.ConradToner.com

Attend any networking function and you're bound to meet a life coach. But what is it that separates the masters from those who are just starting out or have general interests but no in-depth training? How does one pick a life coach? It comes down to this: You have to find one who has the knowledge, real-world life experience and in-depth training that can help you achieve the breakthrough you know you're capable of.

Choosing the right coach requires doing some homework. The best and most productive client/life coach relationships are built on mutual respect, trust and confidentiality. In addition, you want a coach who:

- is passionate and motivated to see you succeed

- has the education, credentials, experience and personality to offer life coaching

- employs scientifically validated personality analysis

- offers complete satisfaction, with a money-back guarantee should you not be satisfied with the coaching program for whatever reason.

Conrad Toner is a master life coach who meets all the above qualifications. More important, he has a track record of helping clients achieve goals they'd only dreamed about.

Before starting a coaching relationship with new clients, Conrad has them complete the Hartman Value Profile (HVP). He uses this scientifically validated personality profile to reveal a person's strengths, natural abilities and weaknesses. It pinpoints thinking preferences and biases and their effects. This allows him to recommend ways to minimize vulnerabilities and work toward a happy, more productive life.

Then, using the HVP as a reference point, the coaching program begins. Conrad offers two programs:

- One-on-One Coaching

- Group Coaching (four to six like-minded individuals)

Organizations and corporations hire Conrad for seminars tailored to meet the specific needs of the group. His seminars include:

- Health, Wealth, Happiness and the Law of Attraction

- How to Make Every Day a Powerful Day

- Be Your Best Self

Conrad is also a certified Law of Attraction trainer.

For additional details on Conrad Toner's coaching programs, seminars and training, visit www.ConradToner.com.

CHAPTER SIX

Finding Happiness When Life Is a Mess

by Judy Palmer

"Happiness depends upon ourselves."
-Aristotle

Are you feeling stuck in a life mess? Do you see your hopes and dreams crumbling before your eyes and think there's nothing you can do about it? Have you tried over and over to pull yourself out of the mess only to find yourself right back where you started? Have you ever caught yourself thinking or saying, "Why bother?" or, "Why does this keep happening to me?" If you answered yes to either of these questions, you're about to experience a dramatic change for the better.

You *can* find happiness when life is a mess!

I'd struggled with panic attacks since I was a little girl. With each traumatic experience that occurred in my life, the attacks became more frequent and powerful until finally they consumed my life on a daily basis. I was diagnosed with panic disorder, agoraphobia, post-traumatic stress disorder and depression. Every area of my life was crumbling. I spiraled out of control and hit rock bottom—hard! And I think the impact shocked me into a new state of awareness.

I was determined to give life all I had one more time. But when I searched inside myself to find something I was passionate about, nothing was there. Tears rolled down my face as I searched in vain for the passionate girl I used to be. I started sorting through my life mess by writing down everything I didn't like about my life and was so overwhelmed that I soon gave up. I remember the voice of frustration and doubt inside me saying, "My life is such a mess. Where do I even start to clean it up? I've tried so many times and failed—what makes me think this time will be different? I have no energy and can't stay out of bed long enough to get routine chores done—what makes me think I can get back on track and change my life?" Does your voice of frustration and doubt say similar things?

Determined to make positive changes but unable to identify anything I was passionate about, I decided that my goal was just to be happy. I was sick and tired of being miserable all the time. All I wanted was to be happy.

If you had told me that simply deciding to be happy would significantly change my life, I probably wouldn't have believed you. But change it did. I noticed a major shift in the very first month! And the change kept happening. Just four months after deciding that happiness was my goal and focusing on participating only in things that made me feel good, I was off all medications, life was getting better by the day and I felt safe traveling alone, panic-free. I felt powerful and happy!

So, yes, I'll say it again: You *can* find happiness when life is a mess! I did it. Thousands of others have done it. And you can do it, too!

Understanding and applying the law of attraction in my life was a key factor in my transformation. I learned that I was unknowingly sabotaging my vibrations and that my overall vibration was congested and contaminated. Keeping my focus on what I really wanted while cleaning up my vibration was very important to creating the changes I desired.

HOW THE LAW OF ATTRACTION IS AFFECTING YOUR EXPERIENCES

"What we think, we become."
-Buddha

The term *Law of Attraction* may be new to some people, but the experience isn't. If you've ever caught yourself using terms such as *coincidence, fate, karma, meant to be,* or *out of the blue,* you're experiencing evidence of the Law of Attraction. Same goes for phrases such as, "When it rains it pours," "A dark cloud seems to keep following me," "If it wasn't for bad luck, I'd have no luck at all." All those phrases are evidence of the Law of Attraction.

The law of attraction states that I attract to my life whatever I give my attention, energy and focus to, whether positive or negative, whether wanted or unwanted. And it has only one job, and that is to match vibrations.

SO, WHAT'S A VIBRATION?

The word *vibration—vibe* for short—has several meanings, but in this chapter, I'm using it to refer to the energy field we create with our mood or feelings. We all have this personal aura, and we also have the ability to instinctively sense it in other people and places.

The thoughts we allow ourselves to think, the words we choose to use and our emotions all create our vibration.

Whatever we include in our energy field, whether positive or negative, wanted or unwanted, we attract more of in our lives. In other words, the results we get are manifested by the vibrations we generate. If we're including good stuff in our vibrations, we attract more good stuff. And yes, if we're including unwanted, yucky stuff that makes us feel bad, we attract more of that, too. We have a vibration for every area of our lives, including our health, career, relationships, finances, spiritual, home, and personal growth. Our *overall vibration* is determined by how we feel about all areas of our lives as a whole.

If you're experiencing a life mess, where bad things keep happening over and over in *all* areas of your life and it seems as if your life is spiraling out of control, your overall vibration may be contaminated.

HOW DOES MY VIBRATION BECOME CONTAMINATED?

Before our vibration becomes contaminated, it goes through the following three-step process:

1. Contrast: Anything that we don't like or doesn't feel good to us. The key is to observe contrast briefly. When

we observe contrast for too long, it can lead to congestion in the vibration.

2. Congestion: Anything that we don't like or doesn't feel good to us that is affecting us mentally and physically. Once our vibration becomes congested in one area, it can begin spilling over into other areas of our life and can eventually contaminate our overall vibration.

3. Contamination: Anything that we don't like or doesn't feel good to us that is affecting our entire life, our overall vibration.

During one of my seminars, a lovely couple named Carol and Ed shared how Ed had been laid off from his high-paying job *(contrast)* and had been struggling to find work *(congestion)*. This job loss caused a lot of stress *(congestion)* in their finances. As time went on, it affected their health and their relationship, as well as their relationships with others. They were also 60 days away from losing their home. Ultimately, the job loss contaminated their overall vibration.

Shortly after attending the seminar, they reported a total shift in their overall vibration. Ed attracted his ideal job, they felt better mentally and physically, their relationship with each other and others improved, they were able to keep their home, they paid their bills and their savings account was growing again.

You may be like me and find that the contamination of your vibration is derived from your childhood. While uncovering my contamination, I learned that panic attacks were the physical, mental and emotional symptoms of my contamination. As

I continued to unravel my experience with the attacks, I found that the actual source of my contamination was my beliefs about death that I had developed as a child. Once I knew this, I was able to heal the contamination at the core, which caused a huge positive shift in all areas of my life very quickly.

Uncovering the 3 C's

Is your vibration congested or contaminated? Let's find out with this exercise:

1. Take a few sheets of paper and draw a line down the middle of each one. (Complete this exercise on the left side of the paper. We'll use the right side in the next section.)

2. Write one area of your life at the top of each paper (finances, career, relationships, health, etc.).

3. Make a list of your contrast—everything you don't like about that area of your life.

4. As you create the list, put an asterisk (*) by any contrast that may be creating congestion. You can tell if it's congestion if you experience a strong negative emotion about it, such as anger, frustration or resentment.

5. Put two asterisks by anything that may be contaminating your vibration and is spilling over and creating problems in other areas of your life.

Hold on to this list. We'll be using the right side of the paper in the next section.

UH-OH, I FOUND SOME CONGESTION AND CONTAMINATION

"Learn to be happy with what you have while you pursue all that you want."
– Jim Rohn, Entrepreneur, Author and Speaker

When my clients find congestion and contamination in their vibrations, the first questions they ask are: What now? How do I clean it up? Where do I start?

First, take a deep breath. It's important for you to understand that creating happiness while cleaning up a life mess is a process. That means there are some things you can do now to create an immediate shift in your life and there are some challenges that may take a little longer. This is particularly true with situations that have been brewing for some time. Always remember that progression beats perfection every time. If you're doing 1 percent better today than you were yesterday, you're making progress.

START BY NURTURING YOUR VIBRATION

I've learned that most people are unknowingly sabotaging their vibration and the results they really want. These people haven't been taught how to take care of their vibration. Have you been taught how to take care of your vibration?

Here are a few things you can do right now to nurture your vibration that will make a significant difference in shifting your vibration from a mess to happiness.

1. Decide to be happy.

Once I decided that my goal was to be happy, I pretended I had a bubble around me. I called it my happy bubble and it represented my life. Envisioning my happy bubble reminded me that only happy things were allowed to be part of my life (my bubble) and it was up to me to design my happy bubble.

Happiness is a feeling. Quite often, we think the law of attraction is only for manifesting material things, resources and people, and while we can do that, I want you to know that you can also manifest your ideal feelings and perspective.

When you catch yourself feeling negative about a situation that makes you unhappy, you have two choices: Let it go or change the way you think about it. Remember, only happy things are allowed in your happy bubble. If something enters your bubble that's unhappy and it must stay temporarily, be deliberate about changing how you think about it. A negative vibration can stop you from manifesting your desires. The goal is to maintain a positive vibration in your happy bubble while you pursue what you really want.

How to Maintain a Positive Vibration in a Negative Situation

Here are a few things you can do to maintain a positive vibration when you catch yourself feeling negative about someone or something you're involved with:

   A. Ask yourself, "So, what do I want? How do I want to feel about this?" Ideally, you'll choose positive words and want to feel good about it.

B. Give attention, energy and focus to creating the feeling you chose. You can give this chosen feeling attention by asking yourself, "How can I perceive this in a positive way?"

C. Make a list highlighting what's great about it. If you look for the bad, you'll find it, and if you look for the good, you'll find that, too. Always choose to maintain a higher vibration by looking for what's good about the situation.

When you change your thinking, you change the vibration you're sending, and remember that the Law of Attraction's job is to match vibrations. Always give the Law of Attraction something good to match.

Action Steps for Today and the Rest of Your Life:

• Create your own happy bubble. This happy bubble is a visual for your life, like the house you live in. The life you're living is *your* life. This is *your* happy bubble.

• Get comfortable and cozy in your happy bubble. You'll be here for the rest of your life. The best part is, since it's *your* happy bubble, you can design and decorate it any way you want to. You can even build on and expand it.

This simple technique will help you maintain a positive vibration while sorting through the things you don't like in your life. Remember, happiness is a feeling, and you can deliberately choose to feel happy about negative situations any time you want to.

2. Take 100 percent responsibility for your life.

After deciding that happiness was my goal and reviewing my life mess by uncovering my 3 C's, I noticed that I had developed a blaming, "poor me" attitude. I blamed everyone else for my mess and allowed outside circumstances and others control over my vibrations and my life. It finally hit me that this was *my* mess, *my* life, just like this is *your* mess, *your* life. You wouldn't lose weight if someone got on the treadmill for you. You have to be the one to get on the treadmill (and actually turn it on).

Are you unknowingly
playing the blame game too?

You can determine whether you're playing the blame game and allowing other people and circumstances to define your life by the way you use these two words: *but* and *because*.

Here are some examples (the italic words indicate where the blame is placed):

- I can't lose weight *because obesity runs in my family.*

- I can't get ahead financially *because of all of my bills.*

- I would be more organized, *but I don't have the time.*

- I can't go to the store *because of my anxiety and panic attacks.*

- I can't focus *because I'm too stressed out.*

- I'd get a job, *but I don't have transportation to get there.*

When a negative statement follows the words *but* or *because*, it's a sign that the area of your life that you're talking about is starving for your attention and that you may be allowing others and outside circumstances to define your life. Always remember, it's *your* life.

Commit to taking 100 percent responsibility for your life, the good and the bad. After all, it's *your* life!

Every time you use the words *but* or *because*, write down what you said. It will help you uncover what's causing you stress and holding you back and allow you to rise above it.

3. Remodel your life

Imagine you were remodeling a house that was in need of major improvements. Each room would need to be de-cluttered and redesigned. When you're experiencing a life mess, cleaning it up is very similar to remodeling a house. Both take time.

Now, Back to the 3 C's List You Created in the Last Section.

On the left side you made a list of all the things you didn't like about your life and uncovered your 3 C's. This is like de-cluttering rooms while remodeling a house. On the right side, you're going to create clarity about what you want instead and redesign your happy bubble, your life, to include more of what you do want.

Let's start with the area that has the most contrast, congestion and contamination.

1. Read the first thing you wrote on the left side of the paper.

2. Ask yourself, "So, what do I want? What would I rather have?"

3. On the right side, write what you want in positive words. For example, if your finances have the most contrast, congestion and contamination and the first thing on your don't-like list is "Not having spending money," what you'll write on the right side is something like "An abundance of spending money."

4. Repeat this process for each thing you don't like, including the other key areas of your life where you found contrast, congestion and contamination.

Once complete, give attention, energy and focus to what you wrote on the right side, take inspired action and live the ideal life you just created on paper.

CHOOSE HAPPINESS TODAY AND EVERY DAY!

> *"A journey of a thousand miles begins with a single step."*
> – Lao Tzu

You can find happiness when life is a mess! Choosing happiness every day and being deliberate about creating your happiness is essential for your long-term fulfillment. The mess wasn't created overnight, so be easy on yourself and allow yourself time to shift and evolve. As you notice shifts and growth taking place in your life, celebrate them. Give the Law of Attraction more good stuff to match.

Rather than being discouraged when you encounter the "old you" along the way, embrace it. When this happens, remind yourself that that's the old you—your old behavior patterns and beliefs—and that you're now forming new behavior patterns and beliefs. You may even feel a tug of war going on between the old you and the new you at times. This is a normal part of the process of creating positive changes in your life. Appreciate the old you for how it has served you while you focus on becoming more deliberate and choosing to continue on your path as the new, happy you.

About the Author

Judy Palmer

Judy Palmer is a catalyst for positive change. Through her dynamic coaching, unique workshops and seminars, she inspires others to transform their lives. As a woman with a down-home personality who has overcome her share of adversity, Judy empathizes with her clients and audience members while empowering them with life-changing wisdom.

Judy has been an award-winning member of multiple leadership teams since 1993. As a dedicated leader, she has trained, motivated and empowered thousands of people in direct sales, business and personal development. Her love of speaking and entertaining audiences emerged while she was a top sales leader in the direct-sales industry for nine years.

While majoring in psychology in college, she discovered her passion for studying the mind, human behavior, personal development and serving others. This passion grew stronger years later after experiencing and overcoming major challenges in her own life. Judy struggled with panic attacks over a 24-year period and was diagnosed with panic disorder, agoraphobia, post-traumatic stress disorder and depression. She was highly medicated and, in her words, felt as if she was "stuck in a life mess."

After committing herself to positive change, she quickly overcame her challenges and transformed her life by implementing the exact steps and strategies she now shares and teaches in her seminars, workshops and private coaching programs.

Driven to continue learning, she attended classes at the Insight Institute in Atlanta and became a certified human behavior specialist in 2010. She embraced Michael Losier's Law of Attraction teachings and became a certified Law of Attraction trainer in 2011. And in 2012, she founded High Vibe Academy.

Judy loves traveling the world inspiring, empowering and teaching others to change their vibes so that they, too, can change their lives.

High Vibe Academy ~ Judy Palmer

"Change Your Vibes, Change Your Life"
www.HighVibeAcademy.com ~ 870-563-6131

Gain instant access to our FREE Change Your Vibes, Change Your Life e-course, current high-vibe training classes and more by visiting www.HighVibeAcademy.com Today!

Services:

- International speaking engagements
- Customized training programs
- Group Coaching
- One to One Private Coaching

Seminars & Workshops:

- Finding Happiness When Life Is a Mess
- Making Peace With Your Past
- Applying Law of Attraction to Your Life
- Making Sense of the Puzzling Patterns of Panic Attacks
- Change Your Vibes, Change Your Life!
- Other Customized Trainings

To connect with Judy and to explore the possibilities of bringing the power of her customized training programs to your group or organization, please visit

www.HighVibeAcademy.com or call 870-563-6131.

WHAT OTHERS ARE SAYING....

"Judy is a great speaker! I have been studying Wayne Dyer, and her training added a lot more to his work in a clearer way."

~Karen, Tennessee

"Love having concrete tools rather than vague platitudes. Great handouts for reinforcement and whole-brain learning."

~David, Tennessee

"Judy is very enthusiastic, knowledgeable and helpful regarding the Law of Attraction."

~ Phil, Pennsylvania

"Judy is a very passionate, positive speaker! Thank you!"

~Deb, Tennessee

CHAPTER SEVEN

Go For the Goal!

by Peter Scott Stringham

Going into the 2012 Olympic Games, Katie Ledecky, a 15-year-old swimmer from Maryland, was not considered a gold-medal contender. She stunned the world when she not only won the gold in the 800-meter freestyle but almost broke the world record. She defeated women who were older and had much more experience in international competition. When she was asked how she did it, she said, "I just started setting some short-term goals and long-term goals and I just blew them away I guess." I was amazed.

She could have attributed her stunning success to any number of things, but the goals she had set were the first thing that came to her mind. Isn't there something we can all learn from this?

Author and speaker Brian Tracy, who has trained more than half a million people and consulted with hundreds of companies, calls goal setting the "master skill of success." He arrived at this conclusion after studying the traits that highly successful people have in common. He studied people who earned success in business, invention, the arts, sports, relationships, politics and being of service to others. He discovered that every successful person he studied was a goal setter. They all set goals for their lives. They set goals for the next five years, for the next year, for the next quarter, for the next month, for the next week and for the next 24 hours. They track the progress of their goals continually. They enjoy the satisfaction of making even the smallest progress toward the achievement of their next goal. It feels good to them to set and achieve their goals, especially that great big one.

Some keep charts and graphs so they always know how they stand toward the achievement of their greatest goal. Some belong to groups that encourage and foster the masterminding of ways to achieve greater success. Some journal. Some write their top goals on cards and look at them throughout the day. Some use visualization techniques to create vivid images that draw their goals to them almost like magic. Some read them into recorders and program their subconscious by listening to themselves talk about their goals while they are in their car, when they are exercising or even when they are sleeping. Some hire coaches to keep them accountable. Some take goal-setting workshops that help them maintain focus and direction. But all of them—all those who live highly satisfying and successful lives—do something purposeful to succeed, and they do it daily. I've yet to meet or read about anyone who doesn't.

I'm not talking about people who are happy having settled for what they have and lie to themselves about living lives of mediocrity. I'm talking about people who have a dream for their lives. In some cases, their dreams were radically different from the lives they were living, but they succeeded against odds to achieve their dreams because they used the supreme power of goal setting.

There are many effective ways to set and achieve goals. Every time I turn around, I hear about another new goal-setting system. But the percentage of people achieving their goals isn't going up. With all the great goal-setting advice that exists, we should all be accomplishing our goals. Instead, most of us fall short. We try one way, it doesn't work for us and we move on. Maybe we didn't learn how to correctly implement the technique Maybe we didn't have a good teacher or coach. There are numerous possibilities, but only one thing that is certain: We didn't stick to it long enough.

I see this every year at the gym where I work out. Right after New Year's, the same thing happens. Starting around 5:15 p.m., the place fills to capacity. The parking lot fills up. There are lines at the most popular workout stations. The throng of folks who have made resolutions to lose weight and get in shape bring the bustle of an airport terminal on a holiday weekend to our peaceful gym. But I don't mind a bit, because I know most of them will be gone in a few weeks. By mid-February, the lines are gone, and we, the regulars, get our gym back. At least for the next 10½ months until New Year's comes again.

We all have our version of "January gym syndrome." It may not be about our health. It may be about what we know we need to do to further our careers, move to a new location or attract the ideal relationship or the ideal life. Why is it that some people stick to their goals and some don't?

I'm about to share a game-changing strategy that works for everyone, regardless of education, experience or skill level. I have read dozens of books, read hundreds of articles and listened to a ridiculous numbers of audios, webinars and classes on the subject of goal achievement, and there's one thing that I've found works every time. And if you implement what I have outlined for you, the next twelve months will be a year of heretofore-unknown levels of happiness because you will experience the joy of setting a goal and seeing it come to fruition. All this thanks to a simple tool that anyone can learn to use and thousands have used with noticeable success. You will be so amazed by what happens that you won't be able to stop yourself from sharing it with others.

There are three steps to my formula for goal achievement:

> Step 1: Define what your goals really are.

> Step 2: Write out your goals using a specific format.

> Step 3: Give your goals attention every day.

STEP 1: DEFINE YOUR GOALS

How can you achieve a goal if you don't know what that goal is? You must have clearly defined goals, and they must be written down. There are dozens of books about how to set goals, and a lot of them are very good. My favorite is *Living Your Best Year Ever,* by Darren Hardy (there's room to write in it, and it comes with a CD). But you don't need a book or an audio to define your goals. You can get started right now—write down some goals, follow the three-step formula, see it work in your life and then, if you still think you need them, use some of the money you're making to buy the books.

Here's an easy way to get started in your goal-achievement practice. (Notice I didn't say goal-*setting* practice. The objective here is not to set goals but to achieve them, so you won't hear me say much more about goal setting.) Get a notebook and make a list of the key areas in your life. Here are some examples:

1. Career: What do you want to do for others that results in being compensated with money or services? Some people call this a job. Write down five things.

2. Finances: How much money do you want to earn, save and invest? What is your net worth, and what would you like it to be?

3. Relationships: What level of satisfaction do you want to experience with the people in your life? *All* the people. This includes significant others, family, friends, business associates, your mailman, everyone. What common threads regarding your relationships with these people can you turn into a goal? Go for five goals now.

4. Health and fitness: What is your definition of being healthy and fit? How much do you want to weigh? Would you like to keep to a program for more than just a couple of months? What are five goals that you could see yourself having fun achieving?

5. Recreation: This word has *re-create* within it. What would work best to return you to your peak of peace, productivity and happiness? It could be a vacation, a hobby or an activity you engage in every day or once a year. I bet it would be easy to write 10 things right now.

6. Physical things you want: Is there anything you want just because it would feel good to have it? You don't need a reason. In fact, it's better not to have one—that's a sign of success! Time to jot down 10 goodies.

7. Personal growth: What would you like to do, be or have that will keep you growing, learning and moving forward in all areas of your life? Write down five.

8. Contribution to humanity: It feels good to help others and to make a difference in your community and in the world. What kinds of things interest you in this area that could become goals for you?

Now you have a nice list of 20 to 30 items that you would like to be, do or have in your life. Next, you need to pare it down and utilize the Law of Attraction to turn your list into a powerful tool that will get you the results you're looking for.

STEP 2: WRITE YOUR GOALS
USING THE LAW OF ATTRACTION

Review your list and select your top 10. Make sure they are your true favorites, not what you think you "should" pick. To maintain more life balance, it can be wise to select at least one goal from each area of life, but that's not a requirement. The most important thing is to do what feels good. This is paramount. If you write down a goal and it feels like a burden or waves of doubt engulf you or you can't see yourself achieving it, leave it off the list for now. If this is your first time writing goals, take it slow—work your way up the goal-achievement ladder one step at a time. If you want to lose 100 pounds but that seems like an impossibility given all the diets you've tried, set a goal to lose 10. That's fine with me and it should be fine with you.

It's much more important to set a small goal and achieve it than to set a mammoth goal and feel like a loser because you get only halfway there.

Now, before you start writing, we have to put in the Law of Attraction piece. The Law of Attraction, about which hundreds of books have been written, states that we draw to ourselves, almost like a magnet, whatever our predominant feelings are about something. Notice that I didn't say predominant *thoughts*. While you have a thought about something before a feeling is generated, it's the feeling that activates the Law of Attraction and brings to you your desires.

Have a great feeling about how wonderful people are and you find yourself surrounded by wonderful people. Have a feeling of joy, accomplishment and high purpose at your job and watch the promotions and raises come your way. If you feel excited every time you look at that magazine with the wonderful photos of the resort in the Caribbean, soon you will find yourself sitting at the beach. I made a booklet of photos from the Caribbean and now I'm being paid to lead seminars there on a regular basis. This is the way the Law of Attraction works for me, and it is the way it will work for you. I promise. Using this technique felt best for me, and as a result, my life became an ongoing vacation.

So what Step 2 is about is activating the Law of Attraction around your 10 favorite goals. The way to do it is to write each goal in the form of a statement that feels good to write down. If it doesn't feel good, write it differently or take it off your list. When writing them down, follow these guidelines so you can get the maximum benefit of the Law of Attraction:

a. The sentence must be true for you.

b. It must be a positive statement, not a negative one.

c. It must be written in such a way that an observer would be able to tell whether you have achieved it. In other words, it must be quantifiable.

d. It must be something you can truly, honestly see yourself accomplishing.

e. You must really want it.

Here's an example: "I love how it feels when I have my ideal partner." It works because:

a. This is a true statement. Notice it doesn't say that I have my ideal partner, only that I love how it feels to have one.

b. It is a positive statement. It's not about ridding ourselves of the partner that doesn't serve us any longer.

c. Someone can observe me with my ideal partner.

d. I can see myself accomplishing this. If I couldn't, I should pare the goal down. I have had people change a goal similar to this one to "I have two dates with the same person." For some that's a big step. Before I met my ideal partner, my goal was to have a relationship that lasted more that six months, something that had never happened before.

e. This is something I really want. This is a subjective issue, to be sure, but if you can't answer yes to this, take it off your list.

Here's another example: "I'm on my way to earning $100,000 in the next twelve months." It works because:

a. We're *all* on our way to earning this much money!

b. Yes, the statement is positive.

c. Sure, someone could theoretically go into my checking account and total all the deposits and see if I hit my goal, whether it's $100,000 or $1,000.

d. I can see this as real for me. If I couldn't, I'd lower the amount. How can you tell if the amount is right? By how it feels. It will take some practice to get in touch with the feeling that the goal is right, but once you have it down, you're on your way to prosperity.

e. Do I really want this? Let me count the ways.

My friend and trainer Michael Losier, author of *Law of Attraction*, also offers some great ways you can begin your goal statements so that it meets the Law of Attraction test:

- I love how it feels …

- I'm on my way …

- I love knowing …

- I'm so excited about …

- I'm excited by the thought of …

- I love the thought of …

- More and more …

- I'm in the process of …

- I love seeing myself …

- I've decided …

So go ahead and write down your 10 favorite goals now. Begin each one with one of the phrases above (or use one of your own), and make sure your statement passes the Law of Attraction test.

How does it feel to write down your goals this way? Does it feel good? Is it enjoyable to imagine yourself achieving each of these goals? If your answer to these questions is "yes," you've "thrown the switch," turning on the Law of Attraction in your life so you can start seeing results like you've never seen before.

STEP 3: GIVE YOUR GOALS ATTENTION EVERY DAY

The third step is easy to learn but takes discipline and commitment to master. I have assigned this exercise to thousands of people. The people who are committed to having more in their lives complete this task and, without exception, get back to me and report amazing results. The promise I make at my seminars is that if you want to double your income in the next year, you will by using this Law of Attraction exercise. I have had people triple their incomes by using this tool. Are you ready?

Make sure the 10 statements you wrote above pass the Law of Attraction test. Rewrite them tomorrow exactly as you wrote them today. Then write them again the next day the same way. And the next day and the next for a full year. No days off. Not Sundays, not Christmas—365 straight days (unless it's a leap year, and then you have to do it 366 straight days).

I know you may have some questions, such as:

1. When is the best time to do this exercise?

   Either first thing in the morning or the last thing before you go to bed.

2. These goals feel really good to write now. What if they don't feel so good after a while?

   At that point, replace them with statements that do feel good, related either to this goal or to some other goal.

3. So it's OK to take a goal off the list?

   Sure. The Law of Attraction is not going to bring your goal to you if you don't have a good feeling about it.

4. What do I do when I achieve one of the goals that I have been writing down?

That is definitely going to happen if you follow this exercise. Lots of times. So when (not if) it does, take it off your list and replace it with a new one, or just write one fewer. That feels good, too.

I wish you success in your quest to achieve all your goals. But more important, I wish you good feelings.

About the Author

Peter Scott Stringham

Peter uses his background in engineering, business ownership and corporate consulting to provide succinct training in the areas of the Law of Attraction, goal setting and achievement, and the fundamentals of living an abundant life.

Peter received a degree in engineering from Lafayette College. He has worked on clean-water projects, co-owned a restaurant, served as general manager of a cable-television company and was an award-winning entrepreneur. Throughout this time, he also studied under many great teachers in the human-potential and sales-training fields. The weekend workshops and Sunday-evening potluck dinners and programs he co-produced with his wife, Carol, at their home in New Castle, New Hampshire, had a steady following. After selling his last business, Peter served as a sales consultant and began pursuing his passion for working with individuals and groups to help them achieve better results in their lives through effective goal setting and goal achievement. In 2006, he met Michael Losier, author of the *Law of Attraction*, and found that Michael's teachings perfectly complemented the teaching he and Carol were already doing. In 2009, Peter became certified to present Michael's signature Law of Attraction workshop, which Peter still presents regularly for clients in the United States and Mexico.

In 2011, Peter and Carol founded Grist Mill Mentors, dedicated to making a difference in the lives of people all over the world. Peter and Carol have found that everywhere they go, people are hungry for the tools that will aid them in living more abundant lives.

Grist Mill Mentors
SEMINARS & COACHING SERVICES

PETER SCOTT STRINGHAM

Peter offers a variety of training and coaching services that provide men and women with tools to awaken their inner power to manifest their desires. With his wife and partner Carol, he has been living and working at the site of a 1600s-era grist mill, where he has been led workshops and provided training services there since 1991. His offerings include:

Training: The use of specific tools that, if applied, will lead to a more abundant and prosperous life is taught in individual and group settings.

Coaching: One-on-one sessions are available to those wishing to have an ongoing coaching relationship.

Online classes and tele-seminars: Check his website for a listing of upcoming programs.

TRAININGS

Your Life Purpose: Clarification of your life purpose and what you are here to accomplish are revealed in this seminar.

The Law of Attraction: Learn the three-step process for activating the Law of Attraction in your life.

Goal Setting Using the Law of Attraction: Learn why so many of us attain goals but don't achieve happy results. Then go through a goal-setting process culminating with an exercise that brings results in all areas of your life.

Your Best Year: Create a blueprint of achievable goals that you are inspired to attain this year in this one-day workshop.

MONTHLY GROUP

Goal Achievement Circle: This group meets in locations throughout New England with a targeted audience consisting of entrepreneurs, salespeople, managers and anyone desiring ongoing support in achieving stated goals.

Grist Mill Mentors
P.O. Box 269
New Castle, NH 03854
603-433-5633
www.gristmillmentors.com

Here's what clients say about Peter:

"You absolutely know the material very well."

"This was the best class I've taken. … The spiritual was embedded in the practical with great tools."

CHAPTER EIGHT

Attracting Your Ideal Weight

by Zaheen Nanji

When I moved to Canada as a teenager, I couldn't get enough fast food. I craved cheeseburgers and devoured french fries. Milkshakes were nirvana. I'd grown up in Kenya, where fast food didn't exist at the time, and my taste buds became addicted to these fatty, fried and frozen delights. My weight increased quickly, and by the time I turned 15, I was a size 14. I didn't like the way I looked, but worse, I didn't like myself.

Determined to make a change, I dived into dieting. I lost 20 pounds on the Scarsdale diet but gained it all back within a year. At 19, I followed Herbal Life and lost 15 pounds but got tired of taking pills every day, so I stopped. I thought I should be able to win this battle without pills. The problem was, I wasn't winning. I wasn't even holding steady. I was gaining.

I wouldn't leave the house without my "butt check" ritual of looking at my behind to make sure my clothes didn't make it look bigger than it already was. I'd given up on finding a miracle skirt that could make it look smaller. At 25 I got married, and before I knew it I'd gained 40 pounds. I didn't realize how big I'd become until I tried to zip up a cocktail dress one evening. I put the dress back on the hanger and reached for my second choice. That one didn't fit either. Within minutes, every dress I owned was on the floor. My husband walked into the room and stopped short when he saw the contents of my closet strewn across the floor. He raised his eyebrows and started to speak but stopped when he saw the fierce look on my face. Slowly backing out of the room, he quietly said, "We have to leave in a half-hour." I forced myself to calm down and finally found a black skirt that would fit if I left the top two buttons open and a jacket that was long enough to hide my unbuttoned waistband.

In the driveway, my husband gingerly asked me if I was okay and I burst into tears. Anger surged through me. "Enough is enough!" I said as I pounded the car. "Nothing fits!" How could I have let this happen? Why did I let it go so far? Without saying a word, my husband wrapped his arms around me and held me while I cried. I felt unworthy and I hated myself. As we drove away, I vowed to do whatever it took to feel worthy again. That realization was the first step in changing my behavior.

In this chapter you will learn the key to mastering the inner game of weight *maintenance*. Anyone who has ever lost weight knows that keeping it off is more challenging than taking it off.

Most people regain the weight and blame the diet. We're missing the point here. Diets are tools for reaching the weight we want to be. They're short-term solutions. It's our responsibility to create a lifestyle that will support our weight maintenance. This is easier said than done, because lasting change requires determination, commitment, practice and the willingness to change some of our beliefs.

Beliefs are the generalizations that form the basis of our reality and guide our behavior. For example, there's a cultural belief among men in certain parts of Africa that being fat equates to being wealthy. Both my father and father-in-law grew up in Africa and said that people paid more attention to them when they'd developed bigger bellies. Since they believed that having a potbelly was a good thing, they chose to eat as much as they could. Being fat or thin carries different meanings for people depending on their culture, belief system and life experiences. Take a few moments now to write your answer to the question: "What does it mean to be fat or thin?"

If beliefs guide our behavior, limiting beliefs hold us back from true success. As Anthony Robbins says in *Awaken the Giant*, "Changing our belief systems is central to making any real and lasting change in our lives."

How do you change belief systems and behaviors about your weight, health and body image? By understanding how you're motivated, aligning your behavior with your values and modeling people who are successful at maintaining weight. These people have empowering belief systems that guide their behavior.

HOW ARE YOU MOTIVATED?

Human beings are motivated toward pleasure or away from pain. Behavioral therapy has shown that people who yo-yo diet are motivated to move away from pain but don't know how to move toward pleasure and stay there.

Have you ever started a diet or exercise program because your clothes were tight or your doctor told you to lose weight? If so, you were being motivated by pain. You were probably thrilled with your initial success, but over time you lost your motivation and slid back to your old habits and behaviors and put the weight back on. People who maintain their weight long-term are motivated by the pleasure of feeling healthy and having a good body image, and they consistently focus on this goal.

As a behavioral weight-loss coach, I ask my clients what they want to achieve and what achieving this goal means to them. By far, the responses I get most are:

- I don't want pain in my joints.

- I don't want to get sick.

- I don't want to shop in specialty clothing stores.

- I don't like being fat and I don't have any self-confidence.

Notice that my clients are answering in negatives and want to move away from pain. But our unconscious mind cannot process negatives, because it interprets everything we say as a positive thought. So if we think, "I don't like being fat," our unconscious minds interpret that as "I like being fat." Our minds do what we direct them to do, so they focus on "liking to be fat" and help us to behave in a way that keeps us fat.

Also notice that when my clients make negative statements, their feelings are negative, too. By thinking about moving away from the cause of their pain, they're giving attention to the very things they don't want. The key to success is to think about what we *do* want and feel good about our decision to achieve it.

To be motivated *toward* what you want requires changing your words, creating new thoughts and behaviors and taking pleasure in moving toward your goals. When my clients share a goal to move away from pain, I ask them, "What do you want instead that is positive and even more important?"

GAINING CLARITY

This exercise will help you tweak your motivation style so that you're moving toward pleasure and can consistently focus on your ideal weight. Draw a line down the center of a sheet of paper. At the top of the left column, write "Away From: What I don't want." At the top of the right column, write "Toward: What I do want." Fill in the left column first. Then, based on what you've written, write what you do want in the right column. For example, if the left column says, "I don't want pain in my joints," the right column might say, "I want to be flexible.

Align Your Actions With Your Values

Just as beliefs guide our behavior, values guide our decisions. Similar to a GPS that guides you to your destination, values drive your behavior based on your decisions. Your values determine the type of career you choose, the friends you have and even the clothes you buy. When our behaviors are congruent with our values, it empowers us to live rich fulfilling lives.

Each area of life has its own set of values. People who struggle with weight are often not clear about what's important to them. To find what you truly value, ask yourself, "What is most important to me?" Once you know what is truly important to you about your weight and health, your behaviors will begin to shift.

Values, Goals and Barriers

Take a few moments to consider your values, become clear about your goal and discover what may be holding you back.

What is important about being at your ideal weight? Write five to ten answers. These are your values.

Sort the values in order of importance, with the most important value at the top. (If you're having trouble sorting the list, visit my website http://www.zaheennanji.com/about-zaheen/value for a more detailed explanation.)

Once you're satisfied with your list, ask yourself if there is a value that you might find useful that is not on your list. Think of someone you admire who has consistently maintained his or her weight and ask yourself, "What would be important to (his or her name)?" Insert that value on your list where appropriate.

Write down your ideal weight and incorporate your most important value into this goal. For example, Mary wanted to be at a weight of 150 pounds, and her most important value was peace, so she stated her goal like this: "I am in the process of being at 150 pounds because I feel more confident and healthier being there, and it gives me a sense of peace."

TACKLING EMOTIONAL EATING

Emotional eating is one of the primary reasons for weight gain. When I ask my clients or workshop participants, "What is the one behavior you would like to change to achieve your ideal weight?" the answer is usually "emotional eating." Emotions trigger us to turn to food, and for some people that has turned into a habit. Behavioral therapy suggests the following three steps for overcoming emotional eating:

Step 1 – Become Aware

When you feel the urge to eat emotionally or engage in behavior that is inconsistent with your weight-loss goals, ask yourself:

- What is making me engage in this kind of behavior?

- How am I feeling and why am I feeling this way?

Step 2 – Find the Positive Intention

The first answers that come to you are the right answers. Some answers may make you blush, cry or gasp, but be prepared to acknowledge those answers. Now ask yourself:

- What am I gaining from this behavior?

- What are the consequences of engaging in this behavior?

I had a workshop participant who binged on sweet foods, especially milk and cookies, at night while the kids were in bed. When I asked her what was making her engage in this behavior, she replied that she was looking for comfort.

"Comfort from what?" I asked.

"I feel things are out of control and it's stressful," she said. "Eating cookies makes me feel better for a while."

"What are you gaining from this behavior other than feeling good?"

"I'm feeling in control."

Notice how a negative behavior for her has a positive intention. Eating cookies made her feel in control, and it's the feeling of being in control that she was craving. I told her to acknowledge these feelings and the positive intention. I finally asked her what the consequences of continuing with this behavior would be.

Her answer: "I will continue feeling upset, I'll gain more weight, but more important, I'll be teaching my kids to numb out their feelings, and I'm scared they will end up like me."

Step 3 – Implement a Plan for Next Time

Life throws us curveballs, and some emotional states may trigger emotional eating. Now that you are aware and recognize the positive intention, plan for those curveballs and devise possible solutions that will be the best fit for you at the time.

Think of specific times when you have turned to food for emotional reasons, and for each time, list at least five actions you could have taken instead of turning to food. Keep this list with you and treat it like a tool in a toolbox.

FIVE PRINCIPLES OF PEOPLE WHO MAINTAIN WEIGHT

Modeling people who are successful at maintaining weight will make you successful! This is the key to human excellence. Since 1994, the National Weight Control Registry has been following more than 10,000 people who have lost significant amounts of weight and kept it off for long periods of time. The registry was created to examine the behavioral and psychological characteristics of weight maintainers and the strategies they use to maintain their weight loss. As a behavioral weight-loss coach, I have also examined the strategies of people who have maintained weight, and if you implement these strategies, you will find success.

Principle #1 – Acceptance

After reaching their ideal weight, people who maintain weight have made an internal decision to continue making healthy choices. That doesn't mean giving up on treats or denying themselves little pleasures, but it comes down to making choices and accepting that this is what they have to do for the rest of their lives. They have chosen to eat low-fat or low-carbohydrate foods and take up particular activities to help stabilize their weight. Acceptance means taking responsibility and ownership of one's weight and health. When we take responsibility, we are determined to succeed because we own the problem.

Principle #2 – Awareness

People who maintain weight notice how their bodies react when they eat something that's good for them and when they slip up and eat something that's not good. For example, if a client has eliminated bread and sugar from her diet, when she eats it, she is aware of the symptoms they trigger such as bloating, lethargy and constipation.

Awareness also means practicing the habit of eating consciously, which includes:

- Allowing the time to enjoy eating.

- Avoiding multitasking while eating and eliminating distractions such as TV and the computer.

- Rating hunger to ensure that you are satisfied but not full to the point of feeling stuffed or bloated.

Principle #3 – Focus

People who maintain weight are very focused on what they want rather on what they don't want. They figure out the consequences of indulging or committing major slip-ups, always keeping in mind the future they want. How do you decide what to order from a menu?

People who struggle with weight base their decisions on the present moment and instant gratification. "I know I should order something light, but the pizza smells too good to pass up."

People who maintain their weight make choices based on how the food is going to make them feel for the next several hours and how it will ultimately affect their health. "I know the pizza is delicious, but I want to have energy for the rest of the day, so I'll have the veggie stir-fry."

This is similar to the motivation styles discussed earlier in this chapter. You begin a diet or exercise program because some kind of pain motivated you to do something about your weight. A month down the road of dieting, you start missing certain foods, and then at a party you're offered a dessert. Everyone is eating dessert and you feel left out and frustrated because you cannot join in the experience. These feelings also cause you pain in the present moment and you want to move away from feeling this way, so you eat the dessert. Instead of focusing on the present, people who maintain weight think about the future they want and consistently make choices to move toward it.

Principle #4 – Feedback

People who maintain weight have admitted to committing major slip-ups and sometimes gaining weight in the process, but they refuse to see it as failure and instead see it as feedback from their body. They have found a different way to approach it. Instead of getting frustrated and giving up on themselves, they have set tolerance levels that allow perhaps 5 to 10 pounds in excess of their normal weight. Once that threshold is reached, they will go back to cutting calories until they reach their daily weight-maintenance goal. To change the way you think about slight weight gains, ask yourself:

1. What do I want?

2. What do I have?

3. What have I learned from this experience?

4. What can I do differently?

5. What will be the evidence of my success?

<u>Principle #5 – Mind-set</u>

Thinking positive thoughts and using positive self-talk is one of the skills that people who maintain weight have said has helped them changed their mind-sets about their weight, health and body image. However, it takes time and practice because people who struggle with weight have programmed their subconscious mind with negative thoughts, and the subconscious mind needs to be retrained with positive thoughts.

Reading or listening to self-development programs, participating in support groups, seeing a professional coach and enrolling in self-development classes are all great ways to attain a positive mind-set and stick to your plan.

TO YOUR SUCCESS

Where do you see yourself five or ten years from now? Feeling the same way—worthless, sad, angry or frustrated? Here's your chance to prepare for successful and lasting change and develop a healthy relationship with your body.

Now that you understand how motivation works and you know the keys to maintaining weight from other people who are successful in this goal, you can start using these tools to help you achieve and maintain your own weight goals for life.

ABOUT THE AUTHOR

Zaheen Nanji

Zaheen Nanji teaches people how to create the lives they want and steers them toward their individual roads to success. Her motto, "Action will lead you to success," was born of her own life experience with overcoming adversity and triumphing over fear.

Zaheen is a success coach, author, professional speaker and owner of Shanti Wellness Centre, in Alberta, Canada. She offers an array of time-tested techniques and powerful principles to propel her clients toward their definitions of success. As a certified coach practitioner, an accredited Law of Attraction trainer and a master in neuro-linguistic programming, she assists people in overcoming fear, changing their inner mind-sets and creating empowering beliefs so they can reach new heights of success.

People who don't know Zaheen's background sometimes assume that achieving success was easy for her. That couldn't be further from the truth. She grew up in Kenya, East Africa, where good-quality higher education was not available and there was little opportunity for economic advancement at the time. When she was 15, her parents bought her and her 17-year-old sister passage to Canada so they could pursue their dreams of knowledge and success.

Although she had stuttered for her whole life and was terrified to go to college, she enrolled at the University of Alberta and earned her Bachelor of Science degree in food sciences and nutrition. Determined not to let her stutter or her fear of speaking stop her, she trained herself to speak clearly with the help of key resources and strategies that she now shares in her workshops and keynotes. For many people who stutter, simply being able to stop stuttering is a dream come true. But Zaheen has *run* with the dream and is now a sought-after motivational speaker.

ZAHEEN NANJI

~Where Transformation and Healing Occur~

4527-56 Street, Wetaskiwin, Alberta, Canada T9A 1V5
Phone: 780-352-0945

Email: info@zaheennanji.com and
info@shantiwellnesscentre.com

Website: www.zaheennanji.com and
www.shantiwellnesscentre.com

Join me on Facebook, Twitter, YouTube and LinkedIn

RADIO SHOWS:

Fat to Thin: http://www.blogtalkradio.com/fat-to-thin

Metamorphosis: http://www.blogtalkradio.com/zaheennanji

SERVICES:

- Speaking engagements and workshops for businesses and organizations

- Private and group consultations

- Nutrition, weight loss and maintenance consulting

SEMINARS INCLUDE:

Attract Your Ideal Weight

This revolutionary one-day program will change the way you think and feel about weight, food and exercise. This is not a diet or exercise program—it's a program to change your behaviors and beliefs about food, health and lifestyle. If you've tried everything and still can't lose weight, Zaheen will help you to identify the unique thoughts and behaviors that *will* work for you.

The Wealthy & Healthy Mind Retreat

This dynamic two-day retreat will change how you think about money and wealth. By understanding your relationship with money, you can shatter your glass ceiling of limitation and transform your life. You'll learn strategies for financial empowerment and find out how to avoid making financial mistakes. Created by leaders in the field of neuro-linguistic programming (NLP), this program is based on years of scientific research. If you're ready to learn cutting-edge techniques for creating the life you want, this workshop is for you.

For more information on Zaheen's services and products, contact her at Shanti Wellness Centre.

CHAPTER NINE

Moving Ahead With Zero-Based Thinking

by Paul V. Xavier

Is something holding you back? Do you feel as if you're on the verge of something great? Have you already achieved success but just can't seem to get to that next level? I know exactly how you feel!

I spent many years frustrated and wondering why I couldn't get my business to the next level. I put in the extra hours and effort, I networked like crazy and I made all the connections I thought I needed to make. But at the end of each year, my business hadn't grown.

During this time I had two business partners, and we all seemed excited about our personal future and the future of our business. We were building a legacy! We would meet on a regular basis, sometimes weekly, to work on our business and make sure we were on the right track. In the early years, we grew by leaps and bounds, with no end in sight. As the years went by, though, the meetings became stagnant and nothing was getting accomplished. We were focused, we worked diligently but we just couldn't get over that hump to really explode our business and take it to the next level.

Still we continued to meet and do what we'd always done: work hard, be honest and network like crazy. But for some reason, nothing was changing. We weren't growing. We had achieved great success that most people would be happy with. We'd made millions of dollars in real estate transactions, trained and helped hundreds if not thousands of real estate investors to get started and grow their businesses, and had a great reputation in our community as honest, reliable, hard-working people. Life was good! The problem was, it wasn't good enough. I wasn't finished building my legacy, but what was holding me back?

I wish I could remember the exact moment when I realized what the problem was and exactly what was said and how I thought I could fix it, but I just don't. I do recall that at one of our weekly meetings, it dawned on me. It didn't knock me upside the head or make me fall out of my seat. It sort of sneaked up on me and whispered in my ear, "You are your own worst enemy. You are holding yourself back." How could that be possible? I put in extra hours and extra effort. I network like crazy. How could I be holding myself back? I had helped to build a million-dollar empire and helped to sustain it over 10 years, so I knew I wasn't a slacker. But I also knew the company had primarily been built in the first three years, and in the seven years that followed, we'd been on a plateau. I reached out to my business partners and we started talking and focusing more on why our business wasn't growing. As we discussed our options, I mentioned again that we were holding ourselves back. We had to figure out how to "break through our glass ceiling".

Is your glass ceiling holding you down? Are you your worst enemy? I finally realized, over time, that my glass ceiling was holding me back. I had to evaluate everything I did from the smallest task to the most complicated and see if my "limited knowledge" was what was holding me back. The fact is, I knew my business inside and out. I knew what I needed to do to be successful, and I'm sure you do, too. And believe it or not, that's part of the problem. I know, it sounds crazy, but here's the problem with being at the top of the food chain: I only know what I know!

It took me some time to realize that I didn't have all the answers I needed. After being a mentor to so many up-and-comers over the years, I had a hard time grasping that I, myself, would benefit from working with a coach to take me to the next level. I now have several coaches and many mentors I talk to and meet with on a regular basis. As a result, my personal life is better than ever and business has exploded. It's amazing!

One of my mentors, J.T. Foxx, closed over $40 million in real estate deals. He then became a serial entrepreneur and started several multimillion-dollar companies and became one the most sought-after motivational speakers. He is also one of the top wealth coaches in the world. And he achieved all this by mastering the art of partnering, branding, networking and marketing. Now that's a legacy!

One of the concepts he talks to me about on a regular basis is "zero-based thinking." The best way I can explain zero-based thinking is through my own experience. The knowledge that helped me achieve a million-dollar empire is not the same knowledge that will help me build a $25 million empire. Doing what I've always done to get where I am is different from doing what I need to do to get where I want to go next. In a sense, I need to start from scratch—from zero.

Zero-based Thinking Takes You to the Next Level

I realize that some of you are thinking that you practice zero-based thinking on a regular basis, and I thought that, too. The problem is that with the limited knowledge we have, even as experts, we see only the things we do from our own perspective and at our own level of knowledge. Instead of going through the practiced motions of our day, zero-based thinking requires us to be conscious of and question every single thing we do.

If you think you already have all the bases covered, try the following exercise, applying it to all aspects of your life, both personal and professional:

1. Evaluate *all* your tasks and processes, or better yet, hire a third party do it for you. When was the last time they were updated/changed by someone other than you or the same person who is responsible for the updates/changes?

2. What tasks are you doing that are second nature to you?

3. Sometimes the saying "Don't fix it if it isn't broken" can be misleading. If you've been doing something for

so long that it feels like second nature to you, chances are you're not questioning how you can do it better and faster. Rethink the choices and tasks that seem obvious. You only know what you know.

4. Consider asking another expert or someone you respect to provide input into what it is you do, both personally and professionally. This can be done by asking about a specific task you're working on, a system you're thinking about implementing or even your business plan as a whole. The key is to get this input from another set of eyes. Are you doing the same thing over and over and expecting different results? This may seem basic, but even the little tasks can make a huge difference in the outcome. If you've been doing something the same way for years, practice forgetting what you know—starting from zero—and approach the task with "new eyes." Ask yourself, "With everything I know and all my life experience, how can I maintain or enhance the quality of the outcome while at the same time making the process more efficient?"

I hope this practical exercise has opened your eyes to the benefits that zero-based thinking can bring to your life. Zero-based thinking works for everyone and is used on a regular basis, though it may not be identified as such. Donald Trump uses zero-based thinking by ensuring he has the right advisers. Michael Jordan used zero-based thinking to increase his skill level in basketball. Just imagine if Donald Trump and Michael Jordan had never risen above doing what they'd done to achieve their first successes. Neither of them would have achieved the success they went on to realize as a result of zero-based thinking.

Brian, one of my coaches, is an experienced and highly successful business professional with a background that ranges from leading large publicly traded corporations to managing a nonprofit organization to building a family business and, now, to owning an entrepreneurial venture. He grew up with entrepreneurs at the dinner table and throughout his career has coached and mentored many business professionals. Brian is the coach who keeps me focused on my task and helps me to see the bigger picture. More important, he helps me to see things I'd have never noticed without zero-based thinking.

During my coaching sessions with Brian, it's his job to help me to see clearly and keep my eyes on the prize. He doesn't say, "Do 'A' or 'B.' " He explains "A" and "B" and then helps me to make the right decision based on what I want. It is crucial that you and your coach are on the same page about what you want to achieve and that you can work together comfortably.

When I'm looking for specific direction, I go to J.T. If I'm stuck on a decision, J.T.'s the guy who will "tell it like it is" rather than coach me through the process. As you decide who you want to coach and mentor you, make sure they know your goals and believe you can achieve them. It's also important for your team to have different areas of expertise, because diversity fosters more growth and development in business, just like in nature. J.T. and Brian are similar in some ways but different in many other ways. J.T. is a self-made entrepreneur who has never worked in the corporate world. Brian climbed the corporate ladder to the top and lived to tell about it. Funny thing is, they're both a perfect fit for me.

As a real estate mentor myself, I have helped countless people achieve success. One of my favorite success stories happened before I knew what zero-based thinking was, but that's exactly what I was doing. I'd flown into West Virginia to work with a young couple I'd been mentoring. They wanted me to spend four days with them focusing on building their real estate business. They'd hit a glass ceiling because their bank wouldn't approve more loans than the two they had. That meant they couldn't get a loan to buy more property until one of the other loans was paid off. Did I mention that Dave and Sue were also college students?

We spent most of the first afternoon talking about what they'd already accomplished, where they wanted to go and how they thought they were going to get there. They owned 12 properties and let me know that they thought they knew at least as much as I did about real estate success. And I can see how they would have thought that.

But what they didn't see was that my road to success had been paved with innovative thinking. They wanted to pay off the properties, but by channeling so much money into that goal, they had a cash shortage and were passing on good deals. Instead of paying off those properties, I explained that they could re-leverage the properties that they owned free and clear. I showed them how to calculate their return on the equity and determined that paying their properties off might not be in their best interest at that time. Now they were listening.

So, part of the problem was solved, but Dave and Sue would still need to raise more capital to invest in more properties and reach their goals for growth. I suggested that they call around to mortgage brokers and make appointments to meet with them. Later in the day, we met with a mortgage broker who assured the young entrepreneurs that they could have more than two loans. Second problem solved.

The couple had thought they had to pay off their properties and couldn't get any more loans. When I provided them with information that made them question what they believed, they burst through their glass ceiling. The only thing holding them back was their limited knowledge. Showing them they could leverage their current properties and actually get loans opened a whole new level of business to them.

I could go on for hours sharing stories about how being open-minded and using zero-based thinking can dramatically change lives. Chances are that you totally get the concept and have seen it used or have used it yourself, maybe without even knowing that's what it's called. What I like about putting the name to it is that it reminds me to start fresh, bring a beginner's mind to the table and find a new and better way to do whatever it is I'm doing.

The key to breaking through your glass ceiling with zero-based thinking is having the right mentor. There are two qualifications that are required of a mentor: The person needs to have succeeded at what you're trying to accomplish, and he or she needs to be willing to help you. Your best friend may be the greatest person in the world, but if he hasn't done what you're looking to do, he's not the best person to give you advice or guidance.

When I decided to write my first book, I sought the guidance of Patrick Snow, author of *Creating Your Own Destiny*. He has a lot of experience with getting authors published and he's willing to help. Perfect match!

FINDING THE RIGHT MENTOR

Here's the process:

1. Determine what it is you want to accomplish.

2. Find someone willing to help. Finding a mentor must be a deliberate and conscious process. Engaging someone to be your mentor isn't always as straightforward as marching into his or her office and asking, "Will you be my mentor?"

3. Attend meetings at an interest-based organization. If you're looking for a real estate mentor, attend a real estate-based organization. Relationships are much more productive if the members are similar in mind-set.

4. Keep in mind that relationships don't respond well to force but bloom beautifully when given space and time to unfold naturally.

5. Start slow and small. Ask your prospective mentor one question and see how he or she responds. You want to find someone who has the unusual and valuable quality of loyalty and continued interest—one who, no matter

what else is happening, will maintain a genuine interest in your continued development.

6. Ask your mentor whether he or she is willing to brainstorm with you. Explain your problem, concern, goal or idea and ask whether he or she has triumphed in a similar situation.

7. Your mentor will probably toss some tasks your way to test your commitment level—be sure to handle them well, as it may determine your future with that mentor.

8. Once you become knowledgeable, pay back the gift you received from your mentor by mentoring someone else. At the same time, never forget you always have more to learn.

As I continue to mentor, I ensure that I continue to be mentored. I can't emphasize enough that the No. 1 reason for my growth and continued success isn't that I have coaches and mentors—it's that I have the *right* coaches and mentors, people who will maintain a genuine interest in my continued development.

I wish I had learned early in life that a great way to become successful is to hang out with the people I want to emulate so I can learn from them. And one of the things I've learned is the greatest piece of advice I can give you: If something needs to be done, just get it done. In one of the first real estate books I ever read, by Russ Whitney, back in 1999, one of his statements made a huge impact on me: "I will do what I ought to do when I ought to do it; no debate." That has stuck with me all these years. Nothing good comes from procrastinating, so just don't do it. It zaps your energy, steals your enthusiasm and creates a vicious circle of not getting things done.

I challenge you to seek out and find a mentor *today!*

ABOUT THE AUTHOR

Paul V. Xavier

Paul V. Xavier is an author, radio personality, national speaker, real estate mentor, entrepreneur, small-business owner, real estate investor, husband and father. He is senior managing partner for Realestate-Extreme, a national real estate-education company that teaches clients how to safely invest in real estate all across the country. Paul is also the founder and president of Hawaii Real Estate Investors, an organization created to foster ethical real estate investing, networking and the education of real estate for investment purposes. Paul is also the principal broker and owner of Nextage Aloha Realty, a real estate brokerage firm located in Hawaii.

Paul is a highly sought-after real estate speaker, trainer, coach and mentor who has worked with thousands of students across the country. He has taught everything from basic real estate classes to advanced strategies such as creative financing, property management and foreclosures. He serves as a personal mentor to hundreds of students across the country and has helped create several millionaires in the process.

Paul is also the founder of the Hawaii Wealth Summit and Think Big Hawaii, annual conferences that focus on business, success and wealth. The Hawaii Wealth Summit, Hawaii's No. 1 wealth-networking conference, features celebrities, industry leaders, millionaires and ordinary people looking to do extraordinary things.

For over a decade Paul has been teaching the same practical applications he uses in his daily life and business activities to help ordinary people accomplish extraordinary things.

REALESTATE-EXTREME

Bridging the Gap Between Theory and Cash Flow

98-029 Hekaha St. #27

Aiea, Hawaii 96701

www.Realestate-Extreme.com

Join me on Facebook, Twitter, YouTube and LinkedIn

Paul V. Xavier founded Realestate-Extreme to empower others through training, networking, brainstorming, motivation and helpful resources about wealth-building principles and strategies. Paul provides quality service by being sincere and honest and creating and delivering valuable information. He listens to the needs of the customer and does whatever he can to create a win-win situation for everyone. Paul's commitment to service is unique in that he truly cares about the community. His belief is that through helping others, all his needs will be met because it is only in giving that we receive. Paul believes that when he conducts his business the right way for the right reasons, the results can only be beneficial for all involved. His philosophy is unmatched by his competitors because it is based on helping others. It is through his commitment to being morally sound that he built the foundation of his company.

STAIRCASE TO SUCCESS:

1. Paul's Home Study Course

2. Paul's Real Estate Immersion Boot Camp

3. Paul's Fast-Track Immersion Mentoring

4. Paul's Gold Immersion Mentoring

5. Paul's Platinum Immersion Mentoring

6. Paul's Elite Immersion Mentoring

BOOKS:

Answering the "What If's" in Real Estate: How You Can Solve any Perceived Problems of Myths When Investing!

OTHER SERVICES:

Hawaii Real Estate Investors: HREI is an affiliation of investors ranging from beginners to advanced, from part-time enthusiasts to full-time professionals. Its purpose is to create an environment that fosters ethical investing, great networking and learning in topics such as locating, buying, financing, renting, managing, maintaining, selling and exchanging real estate for investment purposes. www.HawaiiRealEstateInvestors.com

Nextage Aloha Realty: Unlike traditional real estate companies, Nextage real estate agents offer a professional level of service through a true team-oriented sales process. www.NextageAlohaRealty.com

CHAPTER TEN

Soul Care for
Stressed Superwomen

by Jolina Karen

Stress sucks. It creates illness, destroys marriages and depletes your resources. Surprisingly, it's also your ally. Your anger, frustration, disappointment and fears are your friends, not your enemies. Don't waste them! Your body's ailments and your relationship challenges are messengers, bringing you invaluable information that, when correctly interpreted, can make you stronger, healthier and happier.

All too often, therapies squelch the messenger before the message can be delivered. The messenger is then forced to get louder (more illness or strife), and you have to spend more time and money finding another therapy to silence it. There is a better way: Get the message!

Over the course of my 20-year career as a healer, I have repeatedly witnessed clients successfully uncover the hidden messages in their diseases and bring about significant changes in their health and well-being as a result. I experienced this phenomenon firsthand when I discovered a tumor in my breast. I followed a five-step process that I now call Awakening GRACE ™ and the tumor disappeared. Since that time, I have observed that this process can be applied to every stressor in order to expose the message, awaken our spirit of unconditional love and access the extraordinary healing power of grace.

I would like to invite you to explore three concepts with me. These ideas are foundational to the Awakening GRACE ™ process. While they alone will not complete the process for you, if you're willing to embrace them, they will go a long way toward unlocking the powerful healer within you and show you how to use your stressors to enrich your life.

The three concepts are:

- The real root of your stress has nothing to do with your life.

- There is a brilliant, hidden function in every dysfunction.

- Positive thinking can be disastrously negative to our health, wealth and happiness.

THE REAL ROOT OF STRESS

When I ask women to describe the roots of their stress, they point to things like this: ego, not getting what they need, lack of time, lack of money, lack of direction, demands from others, demands from within, multitasking, lack of control, lack of focus, family pressure, anxiety, and not enough time for everything.

None of these answers really describe the real root of their, or your, stress. The real root of your stress is you. More specifically, your perception of whatever is happening around you causes you to feel stressed. Or not.

Many years ago I attended a retreat on overcoming suffering. The presenter was Father Theofane, a monk from the Snowmass Monastery, in Colorado. The workshop was held in a beautiful home in Vail, Colorado. Fifteen of us made ourselves comfortable in the owner's living room, seated on leather couches, in overstuffed armchairs and on comfy pillows. Father Theofane sat on a kitchen stool. He began his presentation by saying: "I am here. I am seated on a stool. I am fine." He paused, looked around the room and continued. "Now I am looking at you. You're all sitting on big cushions, on couches, in soft chairs. I am starting to think maybe I would be more comfortable if I was sitting over there instead of on this stool. … Now I am suffering."

Your thoughts about your experience, not the experience itself, give rise to your stress or suffering. The experience and the people involved in it have nothing to do with that. You are solely responsible for your interpretation of the stimuli and the stress that you feel as a result of your interpretation.

This may be a very challenging concept for you to grasp. It is for most people. But if you truly want to have a life that is rich and vibrant and nourishing to your soul, it is imperative that you understand this. You must be willing to stop blaming circumstances or other people for your sadness and crediting them for your happiness. Every time you do this, you give your power away, drain your energy and limit yourself to a life of safety and mediocrity.

You are worth so much more than that! You deserve so much more than that. The world around you is waiting for you to see how extraordinary you are so that you can share your greatest gifts with it. And, surprisingly, your stressors (diseases and relationship conflicts) exist to show you what you're not honoring in yourself.

THE HIDDEN FUNCTION IN DYSFUNCTION

We tend to view illnesses or conflicts as dysfunctions that cause us pain and should, therefore, be gotten rid of as quickly as possible. But what if their real function is not to cause pain but to help us avoid pain? What if they are strategies for bypassing or managing deeper pains than we are equipped to face?

Your brain is hardwired to scan for danger. This isn't a bad thing: it's a biologically imperative survival mechanism. It's designed to keep your body alive. When you perceive pain, you will automatically be driven to avoid it and move in the direction of something more pleasurable. For example, if you put your hand into a fire, your pain-pleasure mechanism will instinctively make you pull your hand away and seek something to soothe the burn. If you did not have an aversion to the pain, you would not react the same way. You would feel no impulse to remove your hand. The fire would spread to the rest of your body and you would burn up and die.

Here's the thing: Your brain does not know whether the pain is real (the fire is actually burning your hand) or imagined (you're thinking about your hand burning). It responds to the painful or threatening stimulus in the same way: with a cascade of chemicals—neuropeptides—that initiate a visceral response in your body.

Your body experiences your emotions (mental phenomena) through the same neuropeptides. In other words, your feelings are experienced in your physiology through chemicals. As neuroscientist and pharmacologist Candace Pert wrote, your mental perceptions are experienced in your body via molecules of emotion.

Pain is unavoidable. As long as you have a body, you will experience pains and pleasures. They are the bridge between your inner and outer worlds. Information from the outside world generates sensations in your body that you will label as either good or bad, pleasurable or painful. You need these sensations to give you feedback on your environment. This feedback lets you know you're alive! Think of what it's like when you're asleep. You have no conscious awareness of stimuli coming at you from your environment (the pressure of the blanket, the sound of cars passing by, the smell of rain falling outside your window). In those times, devoid of conscious awareness of pains and pleasures, you are also devoid of the awareness of being alive.

As your mind filters the information coming in from your outside world, it makes judgments about which pains are most important to avoid and which it will live with. In this way you create a hierarchy of pains and, I believe, sometimes create diseases as a way of managing or avoiding the worst of them.

I have observed that disease in the body often reflects three specific dis-eases in the mind. Physical symptoms arise as strategies for managing mental pain. The symptoms perform the strategic functions of helping us get what we want when we don't feel we can allow ourselves to get it any other way; dealing with painful emotions we don't know how to resolve or express effectively; and challenging and invigorating our will to live when we've lost our sense of purpose and can't figure out why we're here.

Let me share some stories to illustrate the different functions of so-called dysfunctions. See if you recognize yourself in any of these scenarios.

Janice is a quintessential 41-year-old superwoman. A successful and sought-after teacher, she organizes volunteers for community initiatives, serves on multiple boards, manages her children's schedules and her family's social life, and is the primary breadwinner in the household.

She came to see me because she was afflicted with debilitating migraines and painful skin rashes. Each time this happened, she'd have to take a few days off to lie in bed and recuperate. When we looked more closely at the timing of her symptoms, she recognized that they always followed an intense feeling of overwhelm and anxiety. "When I hit that breaking point, all I can think is 'Stop the world, I want to get off,' " she said. She desperately wanted to be relieved of the burden of her responsibilities, but she didn't want to let anyone down. Her migraines and skin rashes, we recognized, were giving her an acceptable "out." Some of the main problems or pains her condition helped her avoid were the pains of feeling guilt and shame for not wanting to continue being there for others in the way she had been.

In this next story, Mary's physical symptoms reflected deep anger and frustration that she could not easily resolve. Mary was about 55 years old when she came to see me. As we began our conversation, she blurted out that she was going though an extremely acrimonious divorce that had dragged on for five years. She described her husband as cantankerous and argumentative. Their fights had slowed the proceedings to the point where her lawyer had told her she was not allowed to speak to her husband. This, she said, was so infuriating that she felt crippled. Mary's body was expressing physically what she could not allow herself to express verbally. Her fingers and hands were curling into fists, the neurological symptoms of Lou Gehrig's disease, with which she had recently been diagnosed.

At the subtlest or most essential level, dysfunctions in your body arise from the dreadful inner pain of being unable to identify and live your true purpose, the function for which you were born. The emotional pain that swirls in your mind feels like anxiety, confusion, depression, apathy and boredom. Illness with these roots can be viewed as a strategy for challenging and invigorating your will to live. The deep struggle these diseases can help us to manage is the pain of not knowing how to honor the part of ourselves that wants to be different, assume a different identity and take on more meaningful work. Illnesses at this level are manifestations of the dark night of our superwoman's soul.

Twenty years ago when my mother, Katherine, was ill, I took her to see a woman who had cured herself of cancer. This woman told my mother that the one thing she saw that all her female cancer clients had in common was that they were bored. I was shocked when my mother, a well-respected, busy, philosophy-teaching, circle-dancing, cutting-edge metaphysical healer, said, "You know, you're right. I am bored. I'm tired of being a healer, of doing my work. I feel like I'm waiting for something to pull me forward into life. I just can't figure out what that is."

The function of illness in such cases is to drive us into deep explorations of our innermost longings. It forces us to get in touch with our heart's priorities and the aspects of ourselves that we have been denying in order to create the life we've been living, which no longer feels fulfilling. The pain of the illness can, paradoxically, assist us in breaking the painful addiction to being who we think we are supposed to be.

Which of these three stories resonated with you most? Did you feel a connection to any of the women described here? If so, I encourage you to honor that response. There's something of value in it for you to apply to your own life. I recommend taking some time now to write it out of your body.

WRITE IT OUT OF YOUR BODY

Write a letter to the woman you feel most connected to. Tell her what it was about her story that reminded you of yourself. Describe for her your struggle and share with her how your physical symptoms may be reflecting the emotional pains you're holding inside you. Explore with her how your symptoms may be giving you an "out" of something you don't want to be doing or an "in" to do what you want to be doing but feel guilty doing it. Let her know if you think your symptoms are somehow tied to feeling lost, unsure of your purpose or bored with being the person you've been for so long.

Don't hold back. Let it all out. Don't worry—she won't judge you. After all, she's just like you. And she knows that you, in all your emotional messiness, deserve to be seen and heard. You deserve to be understood. You deserve to be appreciated. This is an opportunity to open up and express what you probably don't often express to many people. I encourage you to write it all out with the intention of illuminating for yourself the hidden gifts or function in your challenge.

Fully letting go with one's emotions, even when by oneself, has become an extraordinarily difficult process for many modern-day superwomen (and men).

Many of us have been conditioned out of giving voice to our anger, blame, hatred, jealousy, insecurity, fears and disappointment. We learned very early on that it was not safe to let loose with our feelings. We were criticized, chastised, told we were overreacting, being too sensitive and that we should somehow be better than that. We believed those messages and took them to heart. Most of us have spent half our lives trying desperately to figure out how to improve ourselves and be of service in ways that assure ourselves that we are good, kind, caring, responsible people worthy of admiration, approval and love. Admitting, even to ourselves, the depth of negativity in our minds is often more than our fragile self-images can handle. The terrible fear that shuts down our hearts and silences our tongues is the fear that the message we received from our primary caregivers, our teachers, the mainstream media, self-help gurus and positive-thinking pundits may be true: By virtue of all the negative emotions in us, we are indeed flawed. This, to me, is a serious concern.

THE DANGEROUS CONSEQUENCES OF POSITIVE THINKING

We can't heal what we can't feel. I believe a major contributor to the unprecedented levels of stress-related illness (both physical and psychological) is not an increase in the amount of pain people are feeling, but rather our growing unwillingness to feel pain.

The truth is, pain and pleasure go hand in hand. We cannot experience one without the other. One of the dangerous ramifications of being besotted with the idea of positive thinking and refusing to feel negative is the death of our spirits. We are meant to feel. Pain is a powerful motivator, an extraordinary teacher and a catalyst for expanding our understanding and appreciation of our higher purpose, our innate strengths and our magnificent inner genius!

Pains give rise to our lives. Without them we would not be who we are. In fact, we would not exist. The secret to healing them lies not in trying to fix or get rid of them but rather in sinking into them, studying them in ever finer detail until their hidden function is illuminated. In that moment of seeing the divine order in what we had previously perceived as pain, our hearts burst open in an experience of the most powerful healing force we know: grace.

Through the stresses and struggles in our own lives, particularly the events that crack our hearts wide open, we are given opportunities to sink into ourselves and come to truly see and hear who we are, to understand the different personas within us, and to appreciate the value of each one of them.

Our stressors are gateways to falling deeply in love with ourselves. When we begin to see the extraordinary brilliance in ourselves, we begin to see it in others. When we begin to see it in others, they begin to see it in themselves. In this way, we change the world.

About the Author

Jolina Karen

Jolina Karen offers assistance with health and relationship challenges to holistically minded people who know there is a deeper meaning to their experience and need guidance to uncover it and heal. "Our diseases and relationship conflicts reflect where we're playing small, giving away our power and not fully honoring our true selves," she says. "As such, they are gateways to falling deeply in love with ourselves."

Having grown up in Africa, where conflict and strife between people were impossible to avoid, her life mission became finding out how we can grow into the highest versions of ourselves, capable of really seeing and hearing one another, understanding our differences and appreciating each other's value.

Through more than two decades of professional practice, Jolina has learned that developing the ability to accept and appreciate others starts with doing the same for ourselves. "Through the strife and struggle in our own lives, particularly the events that crack our hearts wide open, we are given opportunities to sink into ourselves and come to see and hear who we truly are, to understand the different personas within us, and to appreciate the gifts of every one of them," she says. "As we begin to see the wisdom and value in ourselves, we begin to see it in others. When we see it in others, they begin to see it in themselves. In this way, we change the world."

She guides her clients to a deep appreciation for what is *really* going on in their health or relationship challenges so they can free themselves from the drama and activate their mystical, powerful, divinely inspired healers within. She helps her clients to access their extraordinary internal genius and make themselves whole through her transformational healing process, Awakening GRACE™.

Jolina holds degrees and certificates in psychology, sociology, craniosacral therapy, neuromuscular therapy, behavioral kinesiology and the Demartini Method.

JOLINA KAREN

The path to wholeness begins with Grace

P.O. Box 212 Frisco, CO 80443

970-389-4513

jolinak@gmail.com

www.jolinakaren.com

Jolina Karen uses her five-step process Awakening GRACE™ to help holistically minded people find the meaning in their challenges in order to heal. Please visit www.jolinakaren.com to receive a complimentary outline of the process so you can begin applying it in your life.

SERVICES

- Private consultations
- One- to three-day workshops
- Small-group masterminds
- Speaking engagements
- International retreats

SEMINARS

- Awakening GRACE™ for Stress Management
- Awakening GRACE™ for Healing Your Body
- Awakening GRACE™ for Healing Relationships
- Awakening GRACE™ Mastermind

For more details on services and seminars, please visit www.jolinakaren.com.

TESTIMONIALS

"Jolina, you changed my life! I couldn't stop thinking about what you said. I've stopped having panic attacks (after 10 years of being so debilitated by them that she could barely leave the house). I'm now starting my own business and I feel alive again! You're a rock star at what you do! Thank you. Thank you. Thank you." – Ann-Marie, marketing entrepreneur

"Had I not gone down this road with Jolina, I would have been limited to conventional medical treatment for my thyroid condition. I would never have broken the emotional addictions that have been driving my behaviors and draining me. This has given me my power back!" – Sharon, health-care professional

"Having this new structure for thinking about my melanoma has really deepened my understanding of what it's bringing to my life. I already knew that there was good in it, but this has brought me to a whole new level of appreciation. I feel so much lighter and engaged in my life as a result!" – Yvonne, lawyer

Before Jolina .....

Sad
Anxious
Confused
Dissatisfied
Directionless

... after Jolina!

– Joy, artist

Chapter Eleven

Create Heart Centered Prosperity

by Terry Wildemann

Do you believe…

- You are a powerful creator who can manifest positive prosperity in all areas of your life—health, relationships, finances, career and spirituality?

If you answered "no" to the above question, do you believe…

- Life is meant to be a struggle?

- You can't change your circumstances?

- Since you have been unsuccessful in attracting what you really want, the good stuff can't happen to you?

Chances are that I'm on to something here. You see, our parents, teachers, friends, environments and experiences teach us our beliefs. Some of those teachings and experiences are good, and others, well, aren't so good. You know what I mean. Your parents struggle, you witness or experience situations that feel awful, and you become stressed out. If you're an entrepreneur or in a job or career that no longer feeds your soul, you may be living a life of drudgery, resigned to living life just the way it is.

Well, is that really the way it has to be? I don't think so! It's time to change that kind of thinking and heal the negative, fearful emotions that are in your way! Just imagine ...

- Living a life that you deliberately create by establishing goals, devising tasks that will enable you to reach those goals, carrying out those tasks and attracting exactly what you're striving for!

But wait—others have told you that you can't have that. You are not worthy, good, strong, successful or knowledgeable enough. You hate change, you believe you don't deserve it, you fear success or you fear failure. You don't deserve to be happy and no one is going to talk you out of that, right? After all, why should you deserve to be happy, successful, prosperous, the go-to person in your field and living the life you deserve? Why you?

And I say, "*Why not you*?!" You deserve the best life has to offer! You have the tools at your fingertips to attract exactly what you want and get past the fears and emotional blocks keeping you from achieving the success you truly deserve. I will show you how, by working with meridian tapping in tandem with the Law of Attraction, you can achieve your goals with elegance and grace.

Intrigued? Want to learn more? I hope so—people are waiting to meet you because of your talent, knowledge and wisdom. It's time to stop playing small and step into playing the big game of life by working with your vibes in a positive and prosperous way.

You can achieve success, become more positively prosperous than you already are and deliberately create your business and personal life on your terms.

THE GREAT CONTROLLERS: SABOTAGE AND FEAR

How often have you sabotaged yourself? We are all so good at this! We inch forward little by little and are right on the edge of achieving our goals and then—drumroll, please—we do something stupid to ruin it all. We run away. What's up with that?!

Sabotage is rooted in fear, which is a very potent emotion. Think about all the things we have fear about and how hard it is to let go of worrying. Now, you may say, "I don't have any fear!" and I'll tell you to think again. All of us have conscious and subconscious fears. It's part of the human experience. Author and inspirational speaker Esther Hicks uses the word *fear* as an acronym:

F – Forgetting

E – Everything Is

A – All

R – Right

Rate the following fears on a scale of 1 to 10, with 10 being the most powerful emotion:

- fear of losing freedom

- fear of the unknown

- fear of success

- fear of failure

- fear of not being good enough

- fear of disappointment

- fear of lack of money

- fear of not being accepted

- fear of being ridiculed

- fear of making a fool of oneself

- fear of rejection

- fear of not being in control

- fear of not being liked

- fear of change

- fear of not being perfect

Can you think of a few more? Which ones rule your world? There are thousands of fears and you will soon discover that they are at the root of pushing away instead of attracting the positive manifestation you seek. Keep your chin up! You will learn how to shift those fears very soon.

WHAT DOES UNDERSTANDING YOUR FEARS
HAVE TO DO WITH POSITIVE MANIFESTATION?

You may be wondering why I'm spending so much time on helping you identify your fears. And what does all this talk of fear talk have to do with manifestation and the Law of Attraction? Frankly, *everything*! Here's why. When you discover what fears, unconscious blocks and habitual patterns are holding you back from creating the life you desire, you can take action and shift toward deliberately creating positive attraction. Our conscious and unconscious fears create these blocks and patterns. Get it?

Take a good look at your life and you will see a mirror, a reflection of what is going on inside you. The Law of Attraction is all about vibration and mirroring our thoughts, feelings and emotions. Your word choices create positive or negative thoughts that create emotions that have positive or negative vibrations that create your results.

Let's take a good look at the word *attraction*. What words do you see within this word? *At, attract, act, action, traction, ion, on*. These are movement words full of energy. If you dream big and set goals about attracting what you want in life and all you do is sit on a couch without taking action toward those dreams and goals, you get what you get! If you're doing that, how's it working for you? To achieve and attract your dreams and goals, you must take inspired action.

Once you identify and understand the fears that are holding you back, you have the power in your heart and at your fingertips to shift away from them and toward heart-centered success. Fear keeps us from manifesting our very special dreams, goals and desires. The story of Bobbie Jo illustrates how fear can get in the way of success. She ran a licensed home-based day-care business so she could stay at home with her kids. But after a few years, she grew very weary of it. Her children were in school full time and she wanted more. We connected at a women's networking event and she said she was terrified being there, and it showed! She was used to being home with kids. Her handshake was mush, and she had difficulty sharing that she ran a home day care. It was as if she was embarrassed to share her work with people.

Networking was new to Bobbie Jo, and she was highly stressed about the situation. I asked her if she would like to learn a quick stress-relief technique to help her feel more comfortable at the event, and she gratefully said, "Yes!"

BREATHE TO ACHIEVE CALM AND EASE

I asked Bobbie Jo to follow along with a short, simple and powerful three-step process to shift her stress levels:

- Step 1: Shift your attention to the chest area to create body awareness.

- Step 2: Oxygenate the body by breathing deeply and imagining the breath entering and leaving through the chest area.

- Step 3: Think positive thoughts with each breath.

Do this for a few minutes, relaxing your body with each breath. Feel better? I'm sure you do. The better you feel, the easier it is to get into alignment and a state of positive attraction. When

Bobbie Jo finished the exercise, she looked calmer, her face had relaxed and she was smiling.

We chatted a bit and she mentioned that she was tired of her home day-care business and didn't know what she wanted to do. I asked her if she knew about the Law of Attraction and she said she had heard of it. I told her there are three steps to attracting whatever we want and proceeded to explain.

STEPS TO CREATING HEART-CENTERED PROSPERITY

<u>Step 1: Identify what you want—clarity is important to manifesting.</u>

The Law of Attraction gives you what you focus on, and muddy thinking gets in the way of its delivering what you want. Because it's a very obedient law, this foundational step requires crystal-clear focus.

To get clear on attracting her ideal work, I suggested to Bobbie Jo that she use a simple tool that Law of Attraction aficionados use called a contrast sheet. I use this sheet several times a day because it truly creates clarity.

Make Your Contrast Sheet:

1. Fold a clean piece of paper in half.

2. At the top of the left side of the page, write, "What I don't want in a job/career/business."

3. At the top of the right side of the page, write, "What I want in a job/career/business."

4. Write numbers 1 to 20 down the left side.

5. In the numbered spaces, write down exactly what you don't want in a job/career/business. Fill in as many spaces as you can.

6. Look at what you've written and, in the corresponding spaces on the right, write down the exact opposite.

7. Study what you've written. What did you find? Notice common words and phrases.

Below is Bobbie Jo's sheet:

What I don't want in my job/career/business	What I do want in my job/career/business
1. Solitude	Being with people
2. A long drive	20-minute commute—max!
3. Too many tasks	Mix of tasks and interaction with people
4. Working at a desk all day	Doing different and interesting things throughout the day. Maybe traveling or working outdoors.
5. Rude people	Polite and respectful people
6. Working with numbers	Working with people
7. Speaking in front of audiences	Working one to one
8. Office space with no windows	Soothing, nicely decorated office space with windows

9. Being micromanaged	Freedom and flexibility to do my job with a manager who trusts and respects me
10. Inflexible work schedule	Flexible work schedule

Step 2: Give what you desire focused attention—
think about it, feel it, see yourself doing it.

This step is a lot of fun! Use your imagination and visualization skills to mentally and emotionally create your dreams and desires. Fold your contrast sheet in half and begin focusing *only* on what you wrote on the right side. Imagine it all in your mind's eye, giving it detailed focus and energy. See yourself in the job. See yourself working with the great people you want to surround yourself with. Imagine what your office looks like.

Putting the spotlight on the things you want gives them energy and helps you to feel good. The better you feel, the faster you manifest.

Step 3: Allowing—it sounds easy, but it's the
most difficult step of all.

This step is the most important. This is where our control issues and fears get in the way and we self-sabotage. We hold on so tightly out of fear that we don't allow things to fall into place naturally.

Bobbie Jo called the following week to review the exercise. She had filled out several contrast sheets and realized that she wanted to start another business so she could create her own schedule and have the freedom to do what she wanted with her kids.

Bobbie Jo had looked into creating a consulting company for those who wanted to have their own day-care centers in their homes. She had done it for so long that she knew the laws in her state very well and could save a newcomer to the industry lots of time and money with her services and expertise. She was confident that this is what she wanted to do, yet she had an intense edge of hesitancy.

I asked her what her concerns were about starting this business. She was fearful of networking, petrified of being perceived as not knowing what she was doing and scared of the change involved.

Have you ever experienced any of the above fears? I sure have!

The idea of networking sent Bobbie Jo into a tailspin because she did not know what to do when she got to events. Her resistance to networking was huge. It was safer for her to stay in her home doing what she knew than to step out and do what she really wanted to do. How could Bobbie Jo *allow* herself to experience success when these fears held her so strongly? She felt like a failure before she'd even started her new business.

I introduced Bobbie Jo to a brilliant technique called meridian tapping. This powerful and highly effective tool helps reduce stress and diminish fear quickly. It works with the body's energy system much like acupuncture without the needles. Instead we use our fingertips to gently tap on specific body points.

So how does this technique work? Tapping works to realign the body, clearing out the emotional bumps and bruises that affect us. Just like a car that's hit a pothole and is in desperate need of an alignment, our bodies need an alignment as a result of emotional disturbances such as anxiety, fear, anger and grief. These emotions can contribute to physical aches and pains, and the tapping offers relief quickly as the disturbances are healed.

Bobbie Jo was distrusting of this funny-looking technique but was willing to try it. She'd noticed that her headaches were getting worse the longer she stayed in her current business as daycare provider. When she thought of networking, her stomach was turning inside out! Time to start tapping!

Follow the script and tap along. It may look and feel very odd doing this, so I ask that you trust me. The results are worth it. The focus is on clearing the paralyzing fear of not knowing what to do when networking. We will do four rounds.

Round 1: Clearing negative emotions

Karate chop: Use one hand to tap on the karate-chop edge of the other hand.

Say the following phrases while continuously tapping:

- *Even though I am afraid of making a fool out of myself when networking, I accept my feelings.*

- *Even though I am afraid people will criticize and reject me, I love and accept myself anyway.*

- *Even though I hate feeling this out of control and being the center of attention, I accept myself.*

Round 2: Negative round

Tap each of the following points of the body while saying the following phrases:

- Eyebrow (tap inside edge of eyebrow on bridge of nose): *What if I make a fool out of myself at a networking event?*

- Side of eye (tap outside edge of eyebrow): *I know I will.*

- Under eye (tap on bone under eye): *What if people laugh at me because I don't know what I'm doing?*

- Under nose (tap directly under nose): *That would feel awful and embarrassing!*

- Chin point (tap in the cleft of the chin): *Maybe I don't know enough.*

- Collarbone (tap on either side of collarbone): *I'm so afraid I'll make a laughingstock of myself.*

- Top of head (tap on crown of head): *I feel so out of control!*

Take a breath and repeat two or three times. How do you feel?

Round 3: Negative/positive round

Tap each of the following points of the body while saying the following phrases (tap in the same way as in Round 2):

- Eyebrow: *Networking and sales scare me!*

- Side of eyebrow: *I'm scared to make a fool of myself.*

- Under eye: *Why would anyone take me seriously?*

- Under nose: *Why wouldn't they take me seriously?*

- Chin point: *I'm really good at what I do! I've been doing it for years.*

- Collarbone: *I love sharing my gifts with others.*

- Top of head: *Networking allows me to meet great new people.*

Take a breath and repeat two or three times. How do you feel?

Round 4: Positive round

Tap each of the following points of the body while saying the following phrases (tap in the same way as in Round 2):

- Eyebrow: *Networking and sales could really be fun!*

- Side of eyebrow: *I'm learning new skills and meeting nice people.*

- Under eye: *People take me seriously because I take myself seriously.*

- Under nose: *I am a professional and know what I'm doing.*

- Chin point: *I'm really good at what I do! I've been doing it for years.*

- Collarbone: *I love sharing my gifts with others.*

- Top of head: *Networking and sales allow me to meet great new people and grow my business*

Take a breath and repeat two or three times. How do you feel?

ALLOWING PROSPERITY

Bobbie Jo was incredulous at the shifts that she felt. Her emotions were in control, she felt much better about networking and she became clear on how her fears were controlling her. She relaxed and was able to work with her need to control change.

Understanding her fears, tapping and heart-centered breathing became her go-to tools in her growing tool kit. Bobbie Jo often used this magical trio to create positive shifts, and her prosperity grew quickly as she transitioned to consulting full time.

I invite you to follow Bobbie Jo's lead and use these tools daily. They are there to serve and help you grow so that you can play big and share your brilliance with those who are waiting for you to show up. It's your time and you know it. To your success!

About the Author

Terry Wildemann

For Terry Wildemann, understanding how to achieve heart-centered success has been a lifelong quest. Her studies and certifications in the areas of executive and co-active coaching, business, interpersonal communications, stress relief, holistic health and the Law of Attraction, merged with her dynamic world-class professional-development training, coaching and speaking skills, have enabled her to help entrepreneurs and professionals to transform their professional and personal lives. Terry gets to the root of issues quickly, helping her clients to achieve clarity with her seasoned business-building wisdom.

Terry's background includes positions in law enforcement and the hospitality and retail industries, as a CEO and part-owner of a manufacturing company and a career transition trainer to military personnel, as well as 30 years of entrepreneurship. She guides teams, entrepreneurs and professionals into discovering, focusing and communicating their authentic message with her refreshing out-of-the-box coaching and facilitation approach.

With her Shiftology™ Process, Terry shifts her clients into operating their business or career coherently and with new-found insight. The outcome is the discovery of their passion, dynamic goal setting, enhanced decision-making, and improved customer service and communication with co-workers. This process results in reduced stress and the ability to trust themselves like never before, improving performance and increasing profits. Their new heart-centered focus propels them into creating a business or career that truly makes a difference in their lives and the lives of those they wish to influence.

Terry has worked with all branches of the military, banks, chambers of commerce, universities, financial institutions, healthcare institutions, railroad companies, nonprofits and small businesses nationwide.

Terry is the author of *1-800-Courtesy: Connecting With a Winning Telephone Image* (1998 Aegis Publishing) and is a certified executive coach and certified co-active coach, a certified professional behavioral analyst, a certified Law of Attraction trainer, a reiki master, a third-level EFT coach and holds a Bachelor of Science degree from West Chester University.

Heart Centered Success

Provider of Heart-Centered Business- and Career-Building Wisdom

Terry Wildemann, CEC, CPCC
www.Heart CenteredSuccess.com
401.849.5900
HeartCenteredSuccess@gmail.com

Are you an entrepreneur who wants to get off the hamster wheel of life?

What if …

You learned how to *really* work with the Law of Attraction?

Our programs teach you how to work with Law of Attraction to attract more of what you want and less of what you don't want!

You could shift blocks and improve performance?

Meridian tapping, also known as EFT, works with your energy to defuse emotions that get in the way of successful performance.

You trusted your intuition completely?

We are all born with intuition. Some of us learn to work with it well, and others ignore it. Merge it with practical, logical tools and you have a powerful combination that will always serve you in business and life.

You communicated to be heard clearly?

Whether it's employees, co-workers or clients, learning how to communicate how you can help them begins with understanding their "communication" language. We work with the DISC profile to help you understand yourself so that you can understand others and give them what they need.

You can achieve all this and more! Heart Centered Success programs will provide you with business- and career-building tools that will refresh you and transform your business and your attitude. Give us a call to discuss which program is best for you:

- Business Alchemy System 12 week program

- Create Positive Attraction 30 Day Challenge

- Transform Into a Prosperity Magnet workshop

- Heart Centered Inner Circles

- Break Out of Your Shell audio series

- VIP Coaching Days, one-day intense and focused one-to-one coaching

Listen to Terry Wildemann on *Coffee With Terry* on Blog Talk Radio at 1 p.m. Tuesdays as she shares Law of Attraction techniques for business and life. Guests share their success stories and how they merge business and spirituality.

CHAPTER TWELVE

Unlocking Your Power of Perception

by Jeffrey Ferrazzo

I'm going to share with you my four secrets to unlocking your power of perception in this chapter. When I was about 11 years old, my parents shared with me that my mom had suffered through three miscarriages. I'd been their last chance for a second child, and I made it. But why? After talking about this with my mom, my perception about my reason for being alive changed dramatically and started shaping me as a person. Even at the young age of 11, I knew I was supposed to be here. I didn't know what the reason was, but I believed it would be revealed to me in time if I were aware and perceptive. I wanted to be aware enough to notice the opportunities that showed up in my life, and I wanted to be perceptive enough to understand the opportunities I encountered.

Have you ever wondered why certain people come into your life or why you are in someone else's life?

In my early thirties, I came across a story by an unknown author about people coming into our lives for "a reason, a season or a lifetime." I thought it was cool and validating that I wasn't the only one who thought this way. After considering it for a while, I decided that whether someone comes into my life for a season, a lifetime or even just a minute, there must be a reason. Since that time, I've lived this philosophy, and living it has deeply enriched every aspect of my life. This belief encouraged me to go into situations with an open mind, eager to meet interesting people and learn new things. Consequently, I have met some amazing people who have made small and large impacts on my life and helped to shape who I've become. I look at them as my change agents.

One amazing change agent who had a big impact on my life was a Native American named Dave Anderson. Dave grew up in a tough, poor neighborhood of Chicago and had difficulties in school due to his undiagnosed attention-deficit (hyperactivity) disorder. Dave and his mother would spend the summers in northern Wisconsin running an Indian fry bread stand. During those summers, Dave learned to cook. That passion led him into the restaurant business. He became an entrepreneur and humbly opened his first restaurant, Famous Dave's Bar-B-Que Shack, in the small town of Hayward, Wis. The barbecue restaurant did so well that he decided to expand and moved to the Twin Cities in Minnesota. He had amazing success. Along the way, he realized that most of the restaurant managers and staff members were college students and didn't have management or leadership training. So he decided to develop a leadership-training program to teach his managers how to bring out their natural abilities to lead their teams.

The LifeSkills Center for Business Leadership was so successful that even businesses outside the restaurant industry asked Dave to train their corporate managers. With some of the proceeds from their business ventures, Dave and his wife, Kathy, developed a nonprofit version of the center for college students, the LifeSkills Center for Leadership.

Famous Dave Anderson and I crossed paths on a Tuesday in the spring of 2009. He was giving the keynote speech at a local community college my wife was attending, and I went with her to listen to his speech. He described the LifeSkills Center for Leadership Program and shared success stories about the young men and women who had completed the program. And then he said, "There are three spots open for the upcoming weekend, and I will pay the tuition for the next three people who want to attend." My hand shot up. I somehow knew this program would make a difference in my life. During the three-day program, I learned how to raise my level of self-awareness and conquer any adversity within myself in order to emerge stronger and more committed than ever before. I also learned to conquer my fears and overcome my doubts. And I learned that power perceived is the power achieved.

The closing exercise of the program was to write a letter to yourself 90 days out congratulating yourself on the accomplishments you'd made since the training. My letter congratulated me for launching a career as a professional speaker and trainer. I wanted to be able to share the information I have gained over the years with small-business owners.

About 60 days after the event, I "stumbled upon" an opening for the position I now have. I'm a professional speaker and trainer for one of the world's leading online marketing companies and have educated more than10,000 people in the past three years. I am absolutely living the life that I wanted and the life I wrote about in that letter to myself.

I truly believe I am where I am today because I live my life for a reason. I am aware of my surroundings and whom I cross paths with on a daily basis. I am aware of my perception of the opportunities available to me and act on them. When I meet people who say things like "That doesn't happen to me," "I never get that lucky," "I'm never in the right place" or "I never meet those kinds of people," I just don't agree. I believe these opportunities are around us all the time. The key, I've found, is to become more aware of my surroundings and the people I'm meeting. I hone my perceptions and act on the opportunities that are presenting themselves to me.

There are two main reasons that people miss opportunities. Either they're not aware of their physical or social surroundings, or their mind-sets are in the wrong place. They're focused inward on "How does that solve my problem?" or "What's in it for me?"

In my teens and twenties, I was amazed by the ways that people I met could change my life. By my thirties and forties, I found that even more opportunities would come my way if I focused outward by seeing how I or my network of friends and business colleagues can benefit the person whose path I had just crossed. My focus became one of service. I started to question how I could benefit the people who came into my life. How could I be a change agent for *them*? I learned that when we give, we get even more back.

Opportunities are presenting themselves to us all the time through the places we go and the people we meet. This chapter will provide incentive for you to change your mind-set from "What can this person do for me?" to "How can I or someone I know help this person?" or "Who do I know whom this person can help?"

SECRET #1

Expand Your Spatial Awareness

One of the best ways to expand your opportunities is to expand your spatial/social awareness. This will increase the number of people you interact with in any given situation.

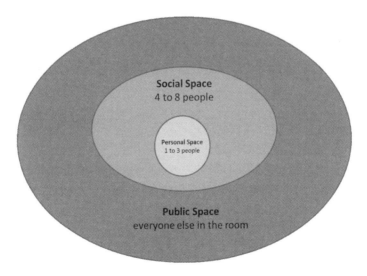

The image above is based on the work of anthropologist Edward T. Hall's personal-reaction bubbles.

People tell me they don't run into enough people or their networks aren't large enough to bring positive effects or blessings into their lives. That may be true, but it's a challenge you can surmount.

Pretend the diagram on the previous page is a reception room at a seminar or party. Do you stay in the circle called Personal Space by creating a little bubble around you that includes only a colleague or one or two acquaintances? If you stay in this space, you won't interact with many new people. You may end up talking as a group to the brave extroverts who wander over to introduce themselves, but at the end of the event, you'll have talked to only a handful of people. Real connections will not be made because real information was not shared. If you stay in your personal space, you usually have polite, superficial group conversations with the visiting extroverts. Group conversations are less likely than one-on-one conversations to reveal how you can serve others or how they can benefit you.

SECRET #2

Expand Your Physical Awareness With Three Simple Steps

1. Visually assess the whole room by making quick observations. This tells you about the host of the event, or it may give you a topic to discuss with the people you are meeting.

2. Scan the room and take note of the people, making quick observations about them, such as: sharp suit, great smile, cool boots—whatever stands out to you.

3. Pick someone who stands out in the most positive way. Or pick someone you've always wanted to meet. Walk over and say hello or sit down next to him or her.

This strategy works for both extroverts and introverts and assures that you meet at least one new person. This will give you a chance to connect with the people you find interesting, and you'll easily double or triple the number of people you connect with outside your normal group.

A little over 20 years ago, I was in the trade-show industry and attended my first national convention. On my lunch break, I noticed a woman sitting at a table by herself, so I went over and asked if I might join her. She welcomed me with this great British accent, and we struck up a conversation. I learned that Susan lived in New York and was a author and presenter. She taught people how to work in a trade-show booth. I thought that was fascinating. I looked at her work as the "software" side of the trade-show industry; I was selling trade-show displays, the "hardware" side of the industry. I saw great synergy between our work. Susan was teaching a breakout session at the conference, and I knew I had to attend. I ended up getting some great ideas that I was able to share with my customers. This helped differentiate me from my competitors and boosted my sales career.

A few years later, I was hired as director of North American sales and training for one of the leading companies in the trade-show industry. One of my first tasks was to revamp the training program for our distributors. I knew right away that I wanted to bring in that great woman who had shared her wisdom with me a few years earlier. The company agreed. So I was blessed to now be working with Susan. We held five training sessions a year for 2½ years, and our work together opened countless doors for both of us.

Years later, when I joined the National Speakers Association, Susan and I ran into each other at a conference, and shortly thereafter she invited me to join in a book project her publishing company, Aviva, was leading. While making a list of potential contributing authors, she thought of me.

All of this bounty for both of us, all reaped from the single act of asking a stranger if I could join her for lunch.

SECRET #3

Be a Good Reporter

My dad taught me to be respectful of everyone I meet. "You never know when you may run into them again," he'd say. I've always been open, willing to talk to anyone. I was always inquisitive, too. My Mom encouraged me to ask questions. "If you want to learn something, ask questions. Pretend you're a reporter," she'd say. These lessons have benefited me throughout my life.

Ask questions and listen intently. We were given two ears but only one mouth for a reason. By listening intently, you honor and respect the person you're speaking with and have a chance to learn something new. I know this isn't easy. I'm a professional speaker and I'm Italian, so I think I was born to talk. Listening with intent takes practice and can be hard work, but the benefits are amazing. I learn something new or interesting from almost everyone I meet. At the least, I have fun and we share a laugh.

As you can imagine, I'm the guy who walks up to strangers and asks if I may have the open seat next to them. When I see people who are alone, I ask if they'd like company. In a crowded restaurant at lunch, I may ask to share your table. And from those small initiatives, I meet people whom my services can benefit, and I meet people whose services can benefit me or someone I know.

SECRET #4

Make Meaningful Connections

Do this exercise at the next social event, workshop or seminar you attend. Practice it until it comes naturally.

1. Introduce yourself, first and last name. Be sure to enunciate and speak clearly. Don't say it fast or mumble—person may feel embarrassed about asking you to repeat it and will hesitate to use your name because you didn't speak clearly. When you share your name, most people will respond by sharing theirs. So listen closely.

2. Repeat names by saying something like "Carol, it's great to meet you." This will help you to remember names.

3. Ask people about their interest or involvement in the event or occasion. "What brings you here?" Listen closely to the answer. Think of what you have in common with them and let them know, "Oh, me, too. I've been looking forward to this presentation for a long time." This helps to establish rapport.

4. Once you know a little about your new contact, introduce yourself and your new contact to someone else. "Hi, I'm Jeffrey Ferrazzo, and this is Doug Wagner. Doug is an editor and book doctor." The new person will then introduce him or herself

and tell me and Doug what he or she does. And inevitably ask me what I do.

Doing this exercise will not only serve you, but it will also enhance the networking in the room, giving more people an opportunity to learn how they can serve others and how others can benefit them. The key is to be your authentic self and be willing to take a risk that can serve everyone involved.

If you're at a conference or seminar and there's a break between sessions or a social hour, select someone you want to talk to and ask him or her what nugget from the past session resonated the most? Or ask what he or she has found to be most interesting at the conference. Commenting on the answer moves the conversation forward and affirms that you're listening.

And don't hesitate to reintroduce yourself to people. Even when I've met people a few times, I'll introduce myself each time until they greet me by name or tell me, "Jeffrey, I remember you, you don't have to introduce yourself to me." Doing this makes sense for two reasons: You don't want them to feel embarrassed if they can't place the name with the face, and you want them to remember you!

I'm so excited about the opportunities and blessings that await you. By increasing your physical and social awareness, you'll notice and open yourself up to the people and opportunities that cross your path daily. I'm confident that if you employ the strategies and tips I've shared, you'll unlock your power of perception. Become a "reporter" and you'll meet some amazing and interesting people. People you probably wouldn't have met otherwise. People who are genuinely talented who may also be able to help others you've met. As a friend of mine says, "Making connections is a beautiful thing." By focusing on how you or someone you know can benefit the people you meet, you can help to create a win-win. I've always enjoyed this quote from legendary basketball coach John Wooden: "You can't have a perfect day without doing something for someone who will never be able to repay you."

I've done training for most of my career, and there was a time when I was on the road four or five days a week, every week, all across North America. I would train up to 20 salespeople and owners every day in sales, marketing and methods for improving their careers and businesses. One day while I was walking through an airport, I heard someone shouting "Jeffrey," but I didn't pay attention to it. I didn't think the person was hollering for me. Then I heard the voice gaining on me. So I turned around and saw a young man chasing after me. When he caught up, he said, "Oh, I am so glad I caught you. I'm late for a flight, but when I saw you I just had to catch up and say thank you and let you know what an impact you had on my life. Going through your training class really opened the doors for me. I've become a tremendous salesperson, a top producer with every company I've worked for since then. I have a great career, a great family and a great home. I can't believe our paths crossed again. I've wanted to thank you for a long time. I have to run. I'm very late for my flight." And he was off.

The information I'd shared had changed his life and he wanted to thank me. That made me feel amazing. In that instant, I knew that all the long hours and miles on the road had been worth it. I was able to help someone improve his life, and that's what business and life are about for me. At that moment, I knew I had become a change agent for someone else and I was fulfilling my life's reason.

ABOUT THE AUTHOR

Jeffrey Ferrazzo

Jeffrey Ferrazzo helps businesses and entrepreneurs initiate and build meaningful professional relationships with individuals and organizations. A small-business marketing expert with more than 20 years of experience, Jeffrey speaks to and trains an average of 3,500 people in numerous companies each year.

As a member of the National Speakers Association, Jeffrey continually develops his use of candor and effective communication to enhance his seminars and keynotes, keeping them fresh and fun. He consistently receives rave reviews from the attendees and organizations that invite him to present.

Jeffrey has successfully launched two small businesses, including one that designed digital-display kiosks for the event-and-tradeshow industry and a consulting firm that trained business owners in sales and sales training, engagement marketing, branding and brand-development strategies.

Jeffrey uses his extensive consulting and training experience to help small businesses, groups and associations maximize the power of engagement marketing.

www.jeffreyferrazzo.com

Jeffrey | Ferrazzo

Are you an entrepreneur or small business owner who needs help navigating the online marketing world?

Do you need to expand your business or non-profit organization's presence through social media, email or event marketing?

If you learned a few secrets about successful networking, could you land more sales or raise more money?

As a professional speaker and trainer for one of the world's leading online marketing companies, Jeffrey Ferrazzo uses his extensive consulting and training experience to help small businesses, groups and associations to maximize the power of engagement marketing. From creating brand-development strategies to sales training, Jeffrey will show you how to initiate and build meaningful professional relationships with individuals and organizations.

To discover what Jeffrey can do for you, visit

Jeffrey Ferrazzo
1670 So. Robert St. #110
Saint Paul, MN 55118
jeff@jeffreyferrazzo.com
www.JeffreyFerrazzo.com

HERE'S WHAT OTHERS ARE SAYING...

"What I enjoy the most about Jeffrey's presentations is his ability to take a complex subject and make it easy for me to understand." Bill from Eden Prairie, MN

"I love the stories Jeffrey shares with us. He makes it so much easier to remember what we came to learn, once we're home or back to the office." Anne from Eau Claire, WI

"Jeffrey is always one of the highest rated speakers we invite in and also the one requested back the most." Bruce from Saint Paul, MN

"One thing I love about Jeffrey is the care he shows to everyone in the audience. He takes time to talk with people individually and then works in specific examples for many of the people he chats with. It's not often a speaker can actually connect with so many people in one session." Christine from Woodbury, MN

Acknowledgments

It takes a village to write and compile an anthology. Thank you to all our significant others, family members, mentors and friends who assisted in the creation and compilation of this book.

Thank you to Michael J. Losier for taking the time out of your full schedule to write our foreword. Your interest and support helped make this book a true expression of our belief in unlocking the power of YOU.

Without a doubt, the dedication and expertise of our support team was invaluable. Thank you to Toni Robino and Doug Wagner of Windword Literary Services for your diligence, thorough project management and brilliant editing; Yael Halpern of Halpern Designs for applying your talents to creating our vibrant cover design; and Shiloh Schroeder and her team at Fusion Creative Works for the beautiful book layout and design.

A very big "thank you" to all of you. We couldn't have done it without you.